Creative
FLOWERS AND PLANTS
FOR YOUR HOME

Cover pictures: (left) The Garden Picture Library/Linda Burgess; (top right) Eaglemoss/Sue Atkinson; (bottom right) Insight London/Michelle Garrett.

Page 1 Clive Nichols; page 3 IPC Magazines/Robert Harding Syndication; page 4 The Garden Picture Library/Steven Wooster; page 5 Eaglemoss/John Suett.

Based on *Creating Your Home*,
published in the UK by
© Eaglemoss Publications Ltd 1996
All rights reserved

First published in North America
in 1997 by Betterway Books,
an imprint of F&W Publications Inc.
1507 Dana Avenue
Cincinnati, Ohio 45207
1-800/289-0963

ISBN 1-55870-470-1

Manufactured in Hong Kong

10 9 8 7 6 5 4 3 2 1

Creative
FLOWERS AND PLANTS
FOR YOUR HOME

BETTERWAY BOOKS

Contents

CREATE INSTANT ELEGANCE WITH CUT FLOWER ARRANGEMENTS

TAKE ONE GLASS VASE

A clear glass vase is worth its weight in gold as the versatile basis for stylish traditional or modern flower arrangements.

Somewhere in the house you're bound to have at least one clear glass vase and, like a blank canvas, it's an invitation to creativity. Depending on taste, decor and budget, you can use almost any combination of flowers and foliage, formal or informal, densely packed or loose and flowing.

Don't expect to achieve the right effect straightaway. Experiment first, to get a feel for the raw material and all of its possibilities. Strong, stiff stems, for example, are valuable for vertical effects, while arching stems add a sense of movement. You can rest heavy flowerheads on the vase rim, or tightly pack flowers so they support each other.

Easy arrangements can be just as stunning as complicated ones. For starters, fill a vase with identical blooms such as a bunch of white lilies; multi-colour blooms of one species such as sweet pea; or mixed flowers in tints of one colour such as pink or gold.

A single peony, phlox and rhododendron blooms with tightly bunched bear grass create a flamboyant effect based on a pink and green theme.

▶ *Combine vivid red carnations in a nest of silvery grey eucalyptus foliage for an easy, elegant display.*

◀ *Roses, honeysuckle and the curious flower-like bracts of euphorbia make up this sweetly scented display.*

INSTANT ARRANGEMENTS

For a fresh, just-picked look, use flowers and foliage from the garden, either on their own or teamed with florist's material.

❖

Wrap a ring of ivy stems round the top of a vase as a living ruffle, with the cut stems in the water.

❖

Fill a vase with ornamental grasses, or a mixture of colourful garden foliage.

❖

Combine long-stemmed florist's roses with fully open garden roses.

❖

Display expensive, single flower stems such as amaryllis, cymbidium or gerbera singly or in pairs, on their own or with a few hosta leaves or fern fronds.

❖

Combine spiky flowers such as delphiniums, larkspur or lupins with a single palm leaf.

❖

Combine florist's roses with a bunch of bear grass or eucalyptus.

◀ *Old-fashioned fragrant roses in pinks and reds make a dense posy in a bowl.*

TIP

SPARKLING CLEAN

When you use a glass vase it's important that what goes below the water line looks good as well as the arrangement of flowers. Always start with a scrupulously clean vase – to shift water marks, stains and sediment from a glass vase, rub with a cut lemon dipped in salt. Remove any leaves below the water line, and arrange the stems with care so that they form an attractive part of the display.

▶ *Luscious poppies contrast with delicate sprays of feverfew and lady's mantle.*

SUPPORTING ROLE

*For a gorgeous cut-flower display that takes no time at all,
arrange your fresh flowers in a glass vase using sparkling coloured
marbles to hold them in place.*

Clear glass vases are delightful containers for cut flowers, showing off their shapes and colours to perfection. But, as with any kind of vase, the individual blooms in an arrangement often need a little extra support to make a really pleasing display. Florists' foam or wire mesh aren't really an option as they don't look very attractive showing through the glass. The answer lies in shimmering glass marbles and brightly coloured stones – not only do they hold the flowers in place but, clustered at the bottom of the vase, they add extra sparkle and style to the arrangement.

You can buy marbles specially made for flower arranging in most florists and department stores. Alternatively, improvise with children's marbles or coloured stones for a different look. Bear in mind the colours in the floral arrangement when you are choosing the marbles. You can pick out a colour in the flowers or go for a striking contrast – this works very well with brightly coloured flowers.

When you are using marbles take care to keep the water in the vase really clean by changing it regularly. Use a cut flower food to ensure a long-lasting display.

The soft pastel shades of a bunch of sweet peas and forget-me-nots look glamorous in an oblong glass tank, half-filled with small clear glass marbles. For very delicate flower stems, it's best to try to arrange the marbles around the stems, rather than pushing the stems in among the marbles.

▼ *Bold green and yellow opaque glass marbles in two different sizes cover the bottom of this tall vase. In combination with the marbles it takes just a few stems of golden yellow ranunculus to make an effective display.*

▶ *With their heavy heads and curving stems, tulips are notoriously difficult to arrange. Here, pearlized glass drops in shades of blue fill the base of an elegant glass vase and help to hold the flowers in place.*

▼ *On a smaller scale, three turquoise tumblers are filled with green glass droplets. They provide enough support to stand one or two stems of Iceland poppy in each glass. Line them up along a shelf or mantelpiece or group them close together on an occasional table for an eye-teasing effect.*

MARBLE CARE

You can use the marbles time and time again, provided you clean them after use. When you are ready to throw away the cut flowers, tip the marbles into a sieve or colander and wash them in a bowl of soapy water. Rinse them well and leave them to dry in a warm place, turning them occasionally. Alternatively, tip them into a soft drying-up cloth or towel and rub them gently. Once they are dry, store them in a strong box or fabric bag.

A BUNCH OF ROSES

Try these quick, easy and eye-catching ways to display florists' or garden roses, as a refreshingly novel alternative to placing them en masse in a vase.

One of the most traditional ways to say it with flowers is to give a bunch of magnificent, straight-stemmed roses. Whether to celebrate an anniversary, birthday or Valentine's Day, or as a way of saying thank you for hospitality, it's sure to please and give pleasure for days to come.

A bunch of roses, however, often arrives when you are at your busiest – preparing the final touches for a dinner party, for example, or just about to go out for an evening – so quickly unwrapping the roses and popping them directly into a vase is very tempting. But if you have just a minute or two to spare, you can create innovative displays that make the most of even a few blooms, to charm yourself, your family and friends. No special equipment or containers are needed – in fact, you'll find everyday household glassware from the kitchen cupboard is very useful, and attractively shaped empty jars have potential as well.

Even if you use the roses full length, always snip off a little of the cut end before arranging, to ensure a steady flow of water to the flower. Remove any leaves that come below the water line so they won't rot.

For an unusual arrangement, strip all the leaves off the roses then cut them so they stand well below the rim of water-filled glass vases. Ordinary, straight-sided glass tumblers are equally suitable – either way, the flowers benefit from the increased humidity within the container.

VARIATIONS

There are countless ideas for charming displays using a simple bunch of roses. A few sprigs of foliage from the garden or snippets from ivy, asparagus fern, weeping fig or begonia house-plant can instantly enrich the blooms. Cutting the stems of the roses so that only a stub remains may seem heretical, but lends the blossom a jewel-like appearance when nestled in a bed of sphagnum or bun moss. Both types of moss are available from florists and keep fresh for weeks – simply keep the moss refrigerated in a plastic bag. Alternatively, you can use the roses as the main ingredient in a more involved display – a formal flower arrangement, swag or fresh flower basket.

▶ *With a little more time and raw materials, you can make roses the focal point of a traditional mixed basket in miniature. Here, rosebuds, ivy foliage and berries and bauble-like white melaleuca are inserted into a saturated florists' foam block, with spikes of pink blossom for contrast.*

◀ *Florists' roses might seem identical at first glance, but they often vary slightly in the curve of the stem and the colour and shape of the flower. Emphasize these subtle differences by displaying the roses individually, cut to different heights, in an artfully arranged cluster of clear glass bottles, carafes and jars.*

▶ *A feast for the eyes – stemless rosebuds in ones and twos, sphagnum moss and tiny sprigs of variegated ivy nestle in a variety of glass dishes, topped up with water. The neutral-toned tray, with its matching, gourd-filled wooden trug, makes for easy transport as well as providing a visual backdrop and boundary for the display.*

ALL WRAPPED UP

*Take one vase, wrap it in fabric held in place
with a showy tie, add fresh flowers, and the result is a
display that's sure to be a real scene-stealer.*

Here's a new approach to flower arranging to bring designer style to even the simplest of displays. Next time you have some cut flowers and would like to try your hand at something different, find a wide-necked vase and wrap it in fabric for a truly inspirational coordinated display.

Wrapping the fabric round the vase couldn't be simpler – no sewing is involved – and you need only a small remnant of fabric, in colours that set off the flowers nicely and work well with the decor and colour scheme of the room.

To keep the wrapping in place, and for an attractive finishing touch, tie a bright ribbon, some coarse cord, a piece of lace or a strip of matching or contrasting fabric around the neck of the vase.

This page shows a heady mix of richly coloured flowers with a coordinating dramatic brocade wrap; overleaf are more ideas to start you thinking.

The top edge of this rich brocade was rolled over, and the raw edges tucked under, to make a fat collar of fabric, with the whole wrapping held in place with silky cord. Flowers used include roses, gerberas, chrysanthemums, veronica and michaelmas daisies.

VASE WRAP

Choose a vase with a neck so that you can tie the fabric in place easily – the rounded glass vase with a fairly wide neck used here is ideal.

Wrap the vase in fabric before you add the flowers. Cut a square of fabric large enough to be gathered up around the vase, with about 7.5cm (3in) to spare. Lay the fabric right side down, stand the vase in the centre and bring the fabric up and round it. Tie the wrapping in place with a coordinating ribbon or cord. Adjust spare fabric above the tie into a pleasing shape – a stiff fabric stands up in attractive peaks, while a soft fabric drapes gently down.

When you arrange the flowers, it may help to use a piece of crumpled chicken wire in the vase to support the stems. An arrangement with a rounded outline works well in the sort of vase shown here. Experiment with different fabrics to suit seasonal flowers – cheerful spots with tulips, bold stripes with hot summer colours, lace for posies of primroses.

Even when there isn't much fresh material around and cut flowers are expensive, you can use just a few florist's flowers and fill out the arrangement with greenery from the garden.

▶ *A sheer fabric was used for this dreamy arrangement – instead of cream organdie, try voile or net. Tie the fabric with string or sea grass, and arrange the folds so the fabric drapes softly down. Shown here is a mixture of roses, wax flower and black-eyed, creamy Ornithogalum arabicum, with white-tipped Euphorbia marginata as foliage. Or try spray carnations and freesias instead.*

▶ *A dramatic arrangement couldn't be easier to get together. You need a vase with a neck, a square of fabric big enough to be gathered around it plus a little extra for neatening, a tie to hold the fabric in place, and a few flowers.*

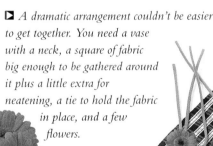

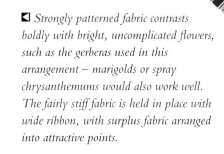

◀ *Strongly patterned fabric contrasts boldly with bright, uncomplicated flowers, such as the gerberas used in this arrangement – marigolds or spray chrysanthemums would also work well. The fairly stiff fabric is held in place with wide ribbon, with surplus fabric arranged into attractive points.*

A DOILY BOUQUET

*Combine a pretty bunch of fresh flowers with a
delicate paper doily to create a sweet, old-fashioned posy
that brightens up any room in your home.*

Wrapping a crisp paper doily collar around a small bunch of fresh flowers is a quick and effective way of creating an eye-catching arrangement. The intricate lace pattern of the doily looks very effective next to small flowers, and the bright white collar contrasts beautifully with the subtle hues of the blooms. A single bouquet in a glass looks great on a mantelpiece or dressing-table. For an even more spectacular effect, make several bouquets with a mixture of colours and group them all together in a large container.

Silver or gold doilies create a glittering effect, but in this style the colour scheme for the flowers must be kept strong, or the doily will dominate the display. Try a green and white scheme wrapped in a silver doily for a sophisticated Christmas arrangement, adding splashes of red for the full festive effect. Yellow, orange and white flowers with a gold doily make a glowing display for a summer celebration.

Four or more single doily bouquets arranged together in a large container make an eye-catching display on a low table. A mixed bunch of coral pink roses, alstroemeria, lace flower and euphorbia creates a summery colour scheme.

MAKING A SINGLE DOILY BOUQUET

Extremely effective, and at the same time inexpensive, this dainty arrangement based on the display shown on the previous page is quick and simple to achieve. You can follow the same three steps to make a posy incorporating flowers of your choice.

1 Tying up the flowers Arrange the flowers in a bunch and then tie the stems together with cotton thread or wire.

3 Shaping the doily Wrap the doily around the bunch of flowers, overlapping the slit edges to form a cone. Pin or tape overlapped edges together.

2 Cutting the doily Using small scissors, cut a slit in the doily from the outer edge to the centre. Then cut out a circle in the centre large enough to take the stems.

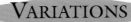

VARIATIONS

For a spring bouquet, try mixing dwarf daffodils, narcissi, grape hyacinths, snowdrops and primroses.

❖

Make a Victorian posy by placing one large flower such as a beautiful full-blown rose in the centre, and encircle it with rosebuds or smaller flowers in a contrasting colour. Finish off with a froth of honeysuckle or a fringe of ferns.

❖

For a summer bouquet in shades of blue try aquilegia, campanula, larkspur, cornflower, and purple asters. You might like to stud the bouquet with a few white daisies or golden buttercups for contrast.

❖

Combine small roses, garden pinks, carnation and sweet peas in the softest shades of blushing pink and cream.

❖

Go for a bright clash of reds and oranges with a dash of black and white. Poppies, chrysanthemums, ranunculus, marigolds, nasturtiums and pansies are good choices.

A fragrant posy of delicate shades of pink and deep red mixed with wispy foliage is prettily enclosed in a double collared gold doily. The gauzy pink ribbon tied in a floppy bow around the neck of the clear glass vase adds a final flourish.

TUSSIE-MUSSIE POSIES

*A traditional aromatic tussie-mussie posy — with flowers chosen
for their symbolic meanings — is a delightful way of creating a pretty floral
display for your home and is perfect as a gift for a special occasion.*

Traditional posies, known as nosegays or tussie-mussies, combine the aromatic scent of herbs with the sweet-smelling fragrance of flowers. Used since medieval days and very popular in Tudor times to serve a practical as well as a decorative purpose, they are imbued with tradition and meaning.

The Elizabethans used them to disguise unpleasant smells and believed they offered protection against infectious diseases – the pocketful of posies in the nursery rhyme has a serious underlying message. Herbs with disinfectant properties, such as lavender, rosemary and rue, were included in the arrangement. The Elizabethans and later the Victorians also turned tussie-mussies to their advantage by playing on the symbolic meanings of various flowers and herbs to convey secret personal messages – especially to lovers.

Each sprig in the bouquet was chosen for its special meaning – roses as a symbol of true love, lemon balm for sympathy and so on.

You can make a tussie-mussie in any size, but a small posy that's easily held in the hand is ideal and simple to create, and adapts well to a variety of simple containers, such as a small jug or bowl. It is inexpensive too, as you need only a few sprigs of each type of flower or herb to make the posy, and you can make use of herbs and flowers from the garden – old-fashioned favourites work best. Traditionally the posy has a rose or another larger flower at the centre with sprigs of other material arranged in rings around it, but if you prefer a more informal look you can simply gather the flowers together more freely, experimenting for the right effect. A doily adds a pretty frill to the posy.

The three traditional tussie-mussies here use readily available flowers, foliage and herbs – cottage-garden favourites are ideal. Ribbons and doilies add attractive finishing touches.

MAKING THE TUSSIE-MUSSIE

Before you start, consider the theme of your tussie-mussie – not only its appearance but also, if appropriate, the message you would like to express. This enables you to select plants for both their appearance and symbolism. For a long lasting display, make sure the flowers and herbs you use are very fresh. If necessary condition the stems and soak them overnight in cold water – see pages 29-30 for more information.

1 Preparing the material Strip any leaves from the lower parts of the stems and remove the rose thorns. With the rosemary as the central point, encircle it with rings of flowers (apart from roses) and herbs, interspersing flowers with leaves for a harmonious effect.

▶ *The ingredients in this tussie-mussie are mainly worked informally with apricot-coloured roses spaced evenly near the outer edges to give the design a touch of symmetry.*

2 Arranging the flowers Hold the posy in your hand and turn it as you work, so you end up with an evenly dense arrangement. When the posy is nearly the required size add the six roses at equal intervals around the outside. Then accentuate the outer layer of the posy with a final ring of assorted foliage and varied plant material.

3 Finishing off the posy Secure the stems of the posy by wrapping them tightly with the florists' tape. Cut the stems so they are an identical length. Place the two doilies at half turns to make eight points and make a hole in the centre. Push the stem of the tussie-mussie through the hole and hold in place with tape. Conceal the tape fixing with a decorative ribbon tied in a bow. Spray the posy with water to keep it looking fresh.

THE LANGUAGE OF FLOWERS

In the 19th century tussie-mussies were given as gifts and tokens of affection, each sprig in the bouquet carefully chosen for what it represented. At its peak the language of flowers was so developed that scarcely a plant was without symbolic meaning – for example, rosemary for remembrance, or oak-leaved geranium for true friendship. A posy of relevant flowers and herbs makes a delightful gift for a birthday or other special occasion – but take care you're not sending mixed messages as some herbs and flowers have double meanings – basil, for example, represents both love and hate.
The following list shows a few examples of the meanings attributed to certain plants:

Angelica – inspiration
Daisy – innocence
Elder – compassion
Fennel – praiseworthy
Forget-me-not – true love
Geranium – comfort
Honesty – honesty
Ivy – fidelity, marriage
Lady's mantle – protection
Lemon balm – sympathy
Lilac – first emotions of love

Lime – conjugal love
Marjoram – blushes
Mint – virtue, purity
Mugwort – happiness
Myrtle – love
Rose – love
Rosemary – remembrance
Sage – domestic virtue
Sorrel – affection
Thyme – courage
Yew – sorrow

SHAPELY DISPLAYS

Use florists' foam to create shaped flower arrangements for stylish displays or to give as gifts. You can buy ready-shaped foam or cut your own design – choose from the three shapes featured here.

Florists' foam is an invaluable material for both fresh and dried flower arranging; the displays here and overleaf couldn't be formed without it. You can buy ready-made foam shapes, such as balls, rings or cones, or cut and shape foam blocks to size.

To make this hanging ball of flowers, trim the chrysanthemum and ivy stems to about 4cm (1½in). Soak the florists' foam ball in water, then tape the end of a length of cord to a thin garden cane and gently push the cane through the centre of the ball, pushing the cord through at the same time. Knot the end of the cord around a 5cm (2in) length of cane to act as a stop, so the cord doesn't pull through the ball.

Use the cord to hang the ball where you can reach it easily, and insert the flowers, spacing them equally and mixing the colours. Fill in any spaces with ivy until all the foam is hidden and then hang the ball in its final position.

A hanging ball of fresh flowers is a delightful way to brighten up a room. You can hang it in a window to enjoy the display from inside and out. A ball this size uses a surprising number of flowerheads, so take advantage of seasonal bargains, such as these chrysanthemums for an autumn display, and use a filler of foliage – in this case, a pretty gold-edged ivy.

HEART SHAPE

This foam-based arrangement is made with mauve Michaelmas daisies, pink carnations, roses and a stem of mauve phlox as a centrepiece. As the flowers are trimmed down, you only need to buy short-stemmed ones for the display. Place the finished arrangement on a solid base – a decorative tray or plate is ideal for a table centrepiece, or set it on foil-covered cardboard if you want to offer the display as a gift. See pages 31-32 for more information on florists' foam.

YOU WILL NEED

❖ PAPER, PENCIL, PINS
❖ SCISSORS and SHARP KNIFE
❖ BLOCK OF FOAM for fresh flowers
❖ NARROW FLORISTS' TAPE
❖ BUNCH OF MAUVE MICHAELMAS DAISIES
❖ TEN PINK CARNATIONS
❖ FIVE RED ROSES
❖ STEM OF MAUVE PHLOX
❖ RIBBON BOW

1 Preparing the foam
Draw a heart shape about 20cm (8in) wide on a piece of paper and cut it out with scissors. Using the sharp knife, cut the block of foam into long sections about 3cm (1¼in) thick.

▶ *You can give this heart-shaped arrangement to someone special, or use it to decorate a celebratory table for an anniversary or Valentine's dinner.*

2 Cutting the heart
Arrange the sections of foam into a flat block and pin the paper template in place on top. Using the sharp knife and following the template, cut through the foam, gradually slicing away to form the heart shape. Carefully remove the paper and pins, taking care not to crumble the foam.

3 Securing the heart
To hold the sections of foam together, stretch lengths of tape across the bottom of the heart. Put the heart shape into a shallow bowl of water until the foam is thoroughly damp.

4 Adding the flowers
Set the heart on a flat plate. Trim the flower stems to 2.5cm (1in) and keep them in water while you arrange them. Working all round the outer edge of the heart, carefully stick a row of Michaelmas daisies into the foam. Inside this, add the carnations, still following the heart shape. Next add the roses, and fill the centre with phlox. Cover the sides of the heart with Michaelmas daisies. Add a ribbon bow, pinned in place, as a final flourish.

◀ *This fresh yellow and white informal arrangement of chrysanthemums and daisies is based very simply on a square of fresh-flower foam. A row of overlapping laurel leaves are pinned in place to cover the sides, with a coordinating ribbon and bow as a pretty finishing touch.*

SUMMER DAISY RING

*Exquisite to look at and easy to make, a ring of enchanting daisies
is an ideal table centrepiece for a summer special occasion. A quick adjustment
turns it into a welcoming wreath for a door or wall.*

As well as looking charming, a circular flower arrangement like a summer daisy ring has great novelty value. A ready-made circular florists' foam base for fresh flowers is crucial to the success of the display. You can buy one in the size you want from a flower shop or florists' suppliers.

To use the ring as a table decoration you can stand it directly on the table or, if the table surface is at all delicate, place it on a mat, large plate or tray. The plastic base that comes with the foam ring should hold in any moisture, but it is wise to take extra precautions just in case.

The colour scheme used here is a fresh combination of blue, mauve and pink with plenty of white to act as a foil. The end result looks extravagant, but it is in fact quite economical to make, as large sprays of flowers are split into single blooms on short stems. The mixture of colours works well, but there are many other options. For a change you can use yellows and oranges with white, or an arrangement with pink, blue and white. Whatever you go for, remember to have some contrast between flowers, so that the individual blooms show up well.

This summer daisy ring looks wonderful decorating a table outdoors for a sunny summer meal or candlelit evening event, but just add a fixing to the back and you can transform it into a welcoming wreath to hang on a door or wall.

MAKING THE RING

1 **Preparing the ring** Soak the ring in a tub or bowl of cold water according to the manufacturer's instructions. Try not to over soak it or it may leak, especially if hung vertically. Stand it in its plastic base.

2 **Preparing the flowers** Cut all the flowers into single blooms or little clusters of florets, so that the stems are about 2cm (¾in) long. Sort them into groups of each type, so you can reach them easily.

3 **Adding the London pride** Start inserting stems of London pride into the foam so that the ring is evenly covered. Keep turning the ring as you add the stems to make sure it looks the same from every angle.

4 **Adding the rest of the flowers** Add the white Michaelmas daisies, again spreading them equally. Repeat for the other flowers, until the ring is completely covered. Turn the ring, checking that it is covered evenly and no foam is showing. Move flowers as necessary until you are satisfied with the look.

TIP
KEEPING IT FRESH
To keep the arrangement looking good for as long as possible spray it occasionally with a fine mist of water.

FORMAL TRIANGULAR DISPLAY

The flowers and foliage in this triangular display fill the space made by three imaginary straight lines connecting three imaginary points. Surprisingly easy to arrange, it adds elegance to a formal occasion.

A floral display should always look lovely in itself, but to be truly successful it must also complement its setting. Triangular arrangements are an unusual and highly effective choice for many formal occasions, from drinks and dinner parties to celebrations such as engagements, anniversaries and birthdays.

Designed to be viewed from the front only, this type of display suits traditional settings, like hall and buffet tables, alcoves and mantelpieces. Wherever the setting, leave plenty of space around the display so you can fully appreciate the simple elegance of the shape and proportions.

To keep the cost down, use plenty of foliage to fill in the parts of the arrangement that aren't directly on show. The display here uses a generous amount of blooms, but owing to its simple geometric symmetry it can look equally effective with slightly fewer flowers.

The colour scheme of this formal triangular display is an unusual mixture of deep coral pink, pale lemon and soft apricot with a subtle background of warm, pinkish green eucalyptus leaves.

MAKING THE DISPLAY

YOU WILL NEED

❖ FLORISTS' FOAM
❖ WHITE BOWL
❖ FLORISTS' TAPE
❖ ASSORTED FOLIAGE,
  1 bunch
❖ EUCALYPTUS LEAVES,
  1 bunch
❖ PINK ANTIRRHINUMS
  (SNAPDRAGONS), 4 stems
❖ TUBEROSES, 3 stems
❖ YELLOW EUPHORBIA
  FULGENS, 3 stems
❖ YELLOW ALSTROEMERIAS,
  3 stems
❖ LEMON CHRYSANTHEMUMS
  2 stems
❖ CORAL PINK NERINES,
  2 bunches
❖ APRICOT LONG-STEMMED
  ROSES, 12 stems

Although the finished triangular display looks very impressive, once you set the limits of size and shape with the first few stems of foliage, the rest of the arrangement is fairly straightforward. Start by setting the height. The usual recommendation is one and a half times the height or width of the container, whichever is the greater, but you can set any height you like, as long as it looks in proportion and is not so high that the display is unbalanced.

Set the overall width about two to three times the height. Gradually fill in the display, working in from the edges. For a pleasing balance, aim for a concentration of heavy, dense flowers and foliage low down and near the centre, with lighter materials towards the edges.

1 **Preparing the base** If necessary, trim the florists' foam block to fit the container. Soak the foam and stand it in the container. Anchor the foam in place by taping across the top in a cross and attaching the tape to the sides of the container.

2 **Setting the outline** Cut the first three stems of the foliage and insert them into the foam to set the height and width of the display. Then cut two shorter pieces of foliage and insert them at the front of the foam facing forwards to set the limit of the display in this direction.

3 **Filling in the outline** Working within and building on the established outline, add the rest of the foliage, including the eucalyptus leaves, and then insert the stems of the antirrhinums in a fan shape, trimming them to the right length where necessary.

▶ *The flowers used in the display are, from top to bottom, yellow Euphorbia fulgens, antirrhinums, roses, nerines, chrysanthemums, alstroemerias and tuberoses.*

4 **Inserting the flowers** Add the tuberoses, euphorbia, alstroemerias and chrysanthemums, trimming their stems where necessary and fanning them out evenly through the arrangement.

5 **Adding the final blooms** Add the nerines to fill out the arrangement, making sure you leave no gaps and that all the blooms are within the established outline. Insert the roses at equal intervals throughout the arrangement. Check the final shape and adjust any flowers as necessary.

ORIENTAL IRISES

*Combine irises, contorted willow branches and
evergreen foliage to capture the elegant, restrained spirit of
traditional Japanese flower arrangements.*

A n arrangement made of just a few flowers, branches and leaves can have as much impact, and require as much thoughtful creativity, as a densely packed one. Indeed, to its devotees, Ikebana – the art of traditional Japanese flower arranging – can be a lifelong study, but you don't need to be a dedicated follower to appreciate its clarity of line and elegance, or to capture its spirit of simplicity in your own flower displays.

On a practical level, Oriental-style arrangements like these irises use few flowers so they are an economical choice and, because the cut stems aren't crowded together, they tend to be long lasting.

Contorted, or pekin, willow (*Salix matsudana* 'Tortuosa'), with its interesting twists and curves, has a particularly Oriental quality. It is available from florists, but you may have to order it in advance. You can use contorted willow time and time again. If you keep it moist it may even burst into leaf, adding a new dimension to the display. Alternatively, you could use hazel or alder branches from the garden, woodland or hedgerow.

Irises also have Oriental overtones but a single variety of chrysanthemum or lily could be used instead. Variegated ivy and Dutch butcher's broom (*Ruscus hypoglossum*), also sold by florists, complete the display; ordinary ivy and butcher's broom (*Ruscus aculeatus*) grow wild in shady, temperate climate woods, and could be substituted.

A simple container in a natural material, such as this plain terracotta bowl, is essential to continue the general theme of understatement and restraint; Oriental shops sell a range of containers specifically made for Ikebana arrangements.

*Irises, ranging from buds that are just
open to full blooms, contorted willow
branches and evergreen foliage, all set
in a simple, moss-filled terracotta
bowl, create an elegant composition
with a strong sense of movement.*

MAKING THE DISPLAY

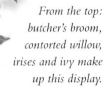

◪ *When composing an Oriental-style display, try to be aware of what are known as the negative shapes – the spaces between the flowers, leaves and branches – created by the positive elements, the actual shapes themselves. Try, too, to achieve an interesting silhouette.*

1 Preparing the florists' foam Leave the foam to soak in a deep container of water until it sinks. Place the foam in the bowl – if necessary, trim to fit. For added stability you can impale the foam on a plastic florists' prong fixed to the base of the bowl with florists' mastic. Cover the foam with sphagnum moss.

2 Establishing dimensions Insert the taller willow branch at the back of the bowl, a little off centre and angled slightly outwards. Cut the second branch about half that height and place it to the side, angled slightly outwards in the opposite direction. Insert the ivy in front, to extend over the rim.

3 Adding the irises Trim the stem of the least open iris to two-thirds of the height of the taller willow, and insert the iris stem vertically in front. Position three half-open irises, in order of diminishing height, vertically in front of the tallest iris, angling the heads in alternating directions, to create a staggered effect.

From the top: butcher's broom, contorted willow, irises and ivy make up this display.

TIP

INSERTING THE STEMS
Always cut stems at an angle when inserting them into foam. If you are using soft- or hollow-stemmed flowers, make a small hole in the foam first with a skewer.

4 Inserting the foliage Shorten the butcher's broom stems to 10-12cm (4-5in) and insert in the base next to the iris stems, leaving space for the final iris.

5 Adding the focal point Cut the stem of a fully open iris to 5cm (2in) and insert between the butcher's broom, facing front. Tease the moss over any exposed florists' foam. Water regularly to keep the foam moist. Once the irises fade you can replace with fresh flowers, if you wish.

THE WAY OF FLOWERS

Originally introduced to Japan from Buddhist China in the sixth century and practised by temple priests, Ikebana – the way or path of flowers – is philosophically based on the six Buddhist principles of energy, concentration, wisdom, patience, morality and generosity. It calls for the minimum amount of material, used with restraint, to create maximum beauty, according to set proportions. In creating these displays, a sense of serenity is achieved, and worldly values rejected. Classic styles include *rikka*, comprising large, vertical displays; and *shoka*, or *seika*, based on an asymmetrical triangle, the three points symbolizing heaven, earth and man.

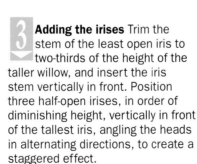

MAINLY FOLIAGE

Use generous amounts of attractive foliage as the mainstay of colourful arrangements, adding just a few flowers, berries or seedpods for touches of extra colour and interest.

The beauty and value of fresh foliage in indoor displays has only recently been fully appreciated. Leaves offer a rich palette of colours, ranging from white through to many shades of yellow, orange, red, purple, blue, bronze, grey and green, with a glossy to velvety matt texture. Their shapes vary from bold and almost geometric to delicate and lace-edged. Aromatic leaves such as Mexican orange and rosemary fill a room with a scent as powerful as any floral fragrance.

You can create handsome, all-foliage displays, but foliage mixed with a few berries or flowers looks even more dramatic. A background of leaves changes one or two blooms – a couple of daffodils, for example, or sprigs of winter-flowering jasmine – into a spectacular arrangement. A few stems of ornamental berries or seedpods such as honesty, Chinese lanterns, rosehips or cotoneaster are similarly enhanced by a backdrop of massed foliage.

Although having your own shrubs and plants to pick from is ideal, florists now stock an increasingly wide range of cut foliage, from traditional box hedge and eucalyptus to elegant, wispy bear grass and exotic palm fronds.

A plain terracotta vase, eucalyptus and two variegated ivies – Hedera helix 'Gold Heart' and the larger-leaved H. colchica 'Variegata' – create a bold setting for sprays of flowering Euphorbia fulgens.

GUIDE TO ARRANGING

Choose the style and colour of the vase or container to suit the foliage and decor. It should be large enough to hold the stems comfortably and balance their weight to prevent the display toppling over.

Support the stems with florists' fresh flower foam blocks, soaked in water first, pinholders, crumpled wire netting or marbles. Alternatively, simply place the stems in the container, heaviest stem first, using each to support the next – branching stems are especially helpful.

Decide whether you want the display to face in one direction or be seen all round. Use the first three stems to set the height and width. Insert more stems to add mass, especially near the centre, and a flow of colour through the display.

◪ *An informal arrangement of green grevillea and mixed eucalyptus with golden honesty seedpods creates a contemporary effect, set in an unusual, bold blue-and-white glazed vase.*

◪ *Glossy, golden-variegated elaeagnus foliage links the cheerful yellow of winter-flowering jasmine and dark green of yew in a sunny, midwinter display, with the bright blue vase providing additional colour.*

◪ *A bright, bold, red-glazed vase sets the tone for this exuberant, early spring display of eucalyptus, Hedera helix 'Gold Heart', cotoneaster berries, red-barked dogwood stems and red chaenomeles or japonica blooms.*

COLOURFUL FOLIAGE OPTIONS

The following are good sources of cut foliage and can either be grown in your garden or bought from florists. Several broad-leaved evergreens, such as Mexican orange, holly and elaeagnus, are available all year round.

White/silver/grey	Yellow	Scarlet/red	Blue/purple	Variegated
Artemisias	Choisya 'Sundance'	Bergenia (in winter)	Hebe 'Autumn Glory'	Variegated elaeagnus
Cotton lavender	Golden-leaved elder	Heather (in winter)	Purple-leaved beech	Variegated hollies
Helichrysum petiolare	Golden-leaved heathers	Maples (in autumn)	Purple-leaved smoke bushes	Variegated hostas
Senecio 'Sunshine'	Golden-leaved hostas	Ornamental rhubarb	Rosa glauca	Variegated ivies
	Golden-leaved privet	Pieris (new growth)	Ruta 'Jackman's Blue'	Variegated phormiums
	Hedera helix 'Buttercup'		Sedum 'Atropurpureum'	Variegated sages

Caring for Cut Flowers

Extend the pleasure of cut flowers with a simple care routine.

A few minutes spent preparing cut flowers guarantees that you enjoy their beauty for as long as possible. The length of time cut flowers stay fresh varies – if they are cared for properly some, such as carnations, can look fresh and attractive for up to three weeks.

When buying or picking flowers, choose carefully. Select stems with buds that are just beginning to open – tightly closed buds sometimes don't open at all. Avoid flowers that are fully open, have loose pollen or dull, drooping leaves. For the best results, prepare flowers and foliage as soon as possible after cutting or buying.

The techniques are quick and easy, and no special tools are needed. Methods vary slightly from one plant to another. Most stems simply need recutting, but others – such as the hard woody stem of a rose – require slightly different techniques which are described overleaf. It's easy to identify the type of stems needing special treatment just by looking at them.

General preparation and care

Recutting stems
As soon as possible after the flowers have been picked, recut the bottom of the stems at an angle to create the largest possible surface area for water to be taken up – to prevent air locks which stop water reaching the flower, do the recutting under water or quickly plunge the stems in water immediately after cutting.

Stripping leaves
Leaves which are submerged in vase water soon rot, making the water stale – remove them when you arrange the display. Also remove dahlia and lilac leaves, which look dull and deprive the flowers of water, and the leaves of chrysanthemum, lily and alstroemeria, which die before the flowers and can spoil a display.

Taking up water
After preparing the stems and removing unwanted leaves, place the flowers and foliage in a deep container of cold water for several hours or, better still, overnight. This completes the conditioning process and makes the flower stems firm and ready for arranging.

Aftercare
Prolong the life of a display by following a few simple steps:
❖ Check the water level daily and top up when necessary – this is especially important for heavy drinkers such as tulips, arum lilies and anemones. With florist's foam, water the foam until excess water overflows into the base.
❖ Change the water completely once a week.
❖ Scrub the container before refilling to stop bacteria forming.
❖ To feed the plants and help keep the water fresh, add cut flower food, or make up your own mix of a few drops of bleach and a pinch of sugar, or a little fizzy lemonade mixed with water.
❖ Recut stems every three or four days, and remove any dead or discoloured foliage.
❖ Keep the display out of direct sunlight and draughts and away from sources of heat such as radiators.
❖ In hot weather or in centrally heated rooms, mist spray hydrangeas, violets and thin-leaved foliage such as ferns.

TIP

ROSE THORNS
Thorny rose stems are difficult to work with and awkward to insert into displays. Florists use special thorn removers, but a sharp pair of scissors work well. Draw the sharp scissor edge along the stem or snip off the thorns individually.

Preparing different stems

To prepare most flowers for display, you need only cut the stems at an angle and remove the lower leaves, as described on the previous page. However, a few easily identifiable flowers will go on giving pleasure for very much longer if you use one of the specific treatments illustrated below.

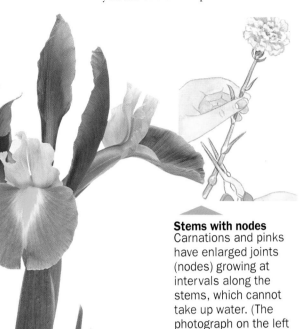

Hollow stems
Delphiniums, lupins and large dahlias have hollow stems. Turn the flower upside-down, fill the stem to the top with water then, with your thumb over the stem end, quickly place the stem in a vase of water. Water will continue to be drawn up the stem, to replace that lost.

Woody stems
Vertically split the bottom 2.5cm (1in) of woody stemmed plants, such as roses or forsythia, to encourage the uptake of water. If the stem is too narrow to split, scrape the bottom 2.5cm (1in). As an extra measure you can also boil the stems (see below).

Stems with nodes
Carnations and pinks have enlarged joints (nodes) growing at intervals along the stems, which cannot take up water. (The photograph on the left shows the nodes on a carnation stem.) For a long-lasting display, recut the stems at an angle between the two lowest nodes.

Milky stems
Plants such as poppies, euphorbias and poinsettias ooze a milky sap when cut. To prevent this, hold the cut end of the stem near a lit match or gas flame for a few seconds then plunge the stem in cold water. (The sap of plants such as euphorbia may cause an allergic reaction, so keep it off your skin.)

Special techniques

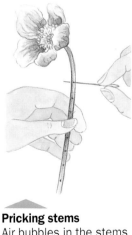

Boiling stems
This can be done if singeing milky stems is difficult – it also helps soften woody stemmed plants, so improving water uptake. Place a towel or paper bag over the flowers to protect them from the steam. Immerse the cut ends of the stems in 2.5cm (1in) of boiling water for a minute, then stand the stems in cold water for several hours.

Pricking stems
Air bubbles in the stems of some flowers, such as tulips, polyanthus and hellebores, prevent the uptake of water. Use a needle or pin to prick the stem just below the flowerheads and at several points down the stem.

Straightening stems
The stems of flowers such as tulips and anemones elongate after being cut and curve towards the light. If straight stems are preferred, roll the stems in newspaper and place them in deep water for several hours.

Reviving wilted flowers
Sometimes flowers, especially roses, show signs of early wilting. If this happens, recut the stem ends and place them in a deep vase of hand-hot water or in 2.5cm (1in) of boiling water for a minute. Then stand the stems in a deep vase of cold water overnight. Wilting roses, hydrangeas, violets and most foliage can be entirely submerged in lukewarm water for a few hours.

Flower Arranging Equipment

With a few basic tools and materials on hand, you can create stylish-looking flower displays with ease.

Instant flower arrangements are created by simply placing flowers in a vase. But when you want a rather more stylish display, there is a wide choice of flower supports available to help you achieve the right effect. For an elaborate dried-flower swag or a formal wedding arrangement, you need various wiring materials. Follow the guidelines given below to equip yourself with everything you need to create any number of displays.

Florists, garden centres and hardware shops sell all the tools and materials – buy the best tools you can afford, as long-term investments.

Flower supports

Give your flower arrangement a pleasing shape by supporting the stems in the following ways.

Florists' foam To hold flowers at set angles, insert the stems into a base of florists' foam. There are two types available.

The green foam is saturated in water for fresh flower displays, while the grey or brown foam is used in its dry state for dried flower arrangements. (Green blocks are too crumbly to use with dried flowers.) To prepare a block of green foam, place it in a sinkful of tepid water and allow it to settle naturally, as it absorbs many times its own weight of water. Do not hold it under the water or a running tap. To check that it is fully saturated, insert a fine skewer or wire into the centre; no bubbles should emerge.

Both types of florists' foam come in rectangular blocks, which you can cut to fit containers of any shape, and as pre-formed cylinders, rings, balls, cones and bouquet foundations with handles. Some have built-in plastic bases, while inexpensive plastic bases are sold separately for blocks and cylinders.

Grey or brown florists' foam can be re-used, though it eventually crumbles. To re-use green foam, wrap the water-soaked blocks in plastic and store in the refrigerator until required. Alternatively, you can dry out damp green foam and re-soak it, though the foam weakens and may crumble.

Florists' prongs For stability, you can impale florists' foam bases on inexpensive plastic prongs.

Florists' mastic Florists' prongs are stuck to the base of a container with oil-based florists' mastic. Mastic only adheres to dry surfaces, and to non-porous, shiny surfaces better than porous or open-weave ones. It is slightly sticky and sold on reels, so store it covered.

Loose supports Glass marbles, pebbles, coloured gravel and similar loose, heavy aggregates look attractive in transparent containers for modern displays.

Pinholders These have tightly packed upright pins on heavy metal bases for impaling stems. They are traditionally part of Japanese-style arrangements when they often form part of the display, but they are also useful for conventional displays. They should be fixed with florists' mastic to the base of a vase and used with mesh to support heavy stems.

Wire netting The most suitable mesh for flower arranging is 5cm (2in) diameter chicken wire. Apart from using it in elaborate dried flower arrangements like plaits and swags, wire netting is loosely crumpled and pushed into containers to support fresh flower stems. As a guide, cut the wire netting twice as long as the vase's width.

The mesh gives less rigid support than florists' foam, but the effect is pleasingly natural. Wire netting is also useful for vases with incurved necks, where it's impossible to use florists' foam. You can wrap florists' foam in an outer layer of wire netting for extra strength in large-scale displays.

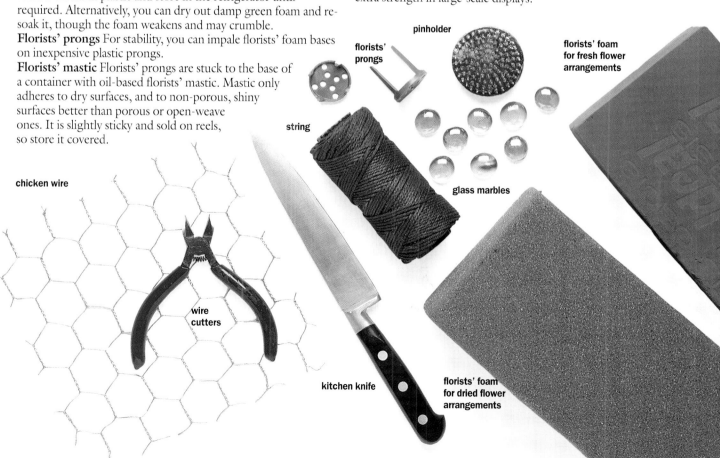

pinholder

florists' prongs

florists' foam for fresh flower arrangements

string

chicken wire

glass marbles

wire cutters

kitchen knife

florists' foam for dried flower arrangements

Cutting implements

Whatever style of flower arranging you prefer, cutting tools are essential for trimming or splicing the stems.

Disposable razors Inexpensive plastic razors are perfect for stripping thorns off rose stems.

Florists' scissors These are very strong and come in various sizes and styles, with pointed or rounded ends. It's a good idea to try them out before buying to make sure that you find them comfortable to use.

Kitchen knives Stainless steel knives are ideal for cutting florists' foam blocks to shape and scraping stems.

Secateurs For cutting thick or woody stems, buy double cutting edge, precision ground, stainless steel secateurs. Try them before buying, to find a pair that feels comfortable, well-balanced and not too heavy.

Wire cutters Although you can cut wire netting or stub wires with florists' scissors, wire cutters are better. To avoid scratches, wear gardening gloves when cutting wire mesh.

florists' scissors

florists' mastic

secateurs

reel wire

Wiring materials

Wire is a vital component of many formal dried and fresh flower arrangments.

Florists' tape Sometimes referred to as gutta-percha, this green or brown tape is used to conceal wired stems.

Florists' wire Reel wire is made of heated and slowly cooled, or annealed, steel; finer reel rose wire is made of tin-coated steel. Both are used for binding wired stems, making garlands and tying mesh netting in position. Reel rose wire is also used for wiring florets into tiny bunches. If buying only one reel, choose a medium gauge, 24SWG (Standard Wire Gauge).

Stub wires Sold in individual lengths, stub wires are used to support weak or hollow stems. They vary from 15-40cm (6-16in) long and in thickness and strength from 36-18SWG. (The lower the gauge number, the thicker the wire.) If buying only one type of stub wire, go for a medium, 22 or 24SWG gauge.

stub wires

florists' tape

Sensible extras

Buckets Deep buckets are indispensable for conditioning fresh flowers and storing bunches of dried flowers.

Plastic sheeting Spread plastic sheeting over the floor when arranging flowers in a carpeted area. *Dust sheets* save time and mess if you are working with dried flowers, which shed bits and pieces everywhere.

String Three or four ply medium fillis is sturdy and flexible. Raffia and natural jute fillis are also not only strong and flexible, but attractive as well – an important factor if they form part of the finished display.

Containers

Your choice of container is virtually infinite, and crucial to the success of the arrangement. Not only does it hold the flowers, but it also suggests the best shape and colour scheme for the display.

Baskets are particularly suitable for dried flower arrangements. Shopping baskets, bicycle baskets or bread baskets work equally well. Smaller baskets need to be weighted down with pebbles to prevent the arrangement toppling over.

A candlecup is a shallow plastic bowl with a short stem that fits into the top of a candlestick. When filled with a block of florists' foam, it supports an arrangement round the base of a candle.

Ceramic vases in a bewildering variety of colours, sizes and shapes abound, from the tall and upright, to a shallow bowl or a narrow-necked urn. Some are patterned, others plain. A white or earthy shade is a good all-purpose choice. Don't hesitate to improvise; a teapot, a fluted soufflé dish or a tiny eggcup make excellent stand-ins for smaller arrangements; a large china jug does stalwart service for big bouquets.

Glass vases are just as versatile as ceramic ones, as long as they are sparkling clean, the flower water is freshened regularly and the visible stems look attractive. A chipped wine glass or a sugar bowl forms a good basis for a small, informal arrangement.

Metal jugs, bowls or **boxes** made of copper, brass and silver look lovely filled with fresh or dried flowers. If the container has seams, check that it is watertight before arranging any fresh flowers.

Novelty containers with unusual shapes often inspire creative designs. Many natural or everyday objects have potential as receptacles for flower arrangments – jam jars, shells or hollowed-out vegetables spring to mind.

Plastic versions of many container shapes are available at most florists. They are unbreakable and easily transportable, but rather unstable unless you weight the base with heavy plaster filler.

Wall-mounted vases have flat backs so that they lie straight and level on the wall, with flowers and foliage tumbling down over the front.

Preserving Flowers

Drying or preserving your own flowers and foliage allows you to create long-lasting flower displays with a personal touch.

The three traditional techniques for drying or preserving flowers and foliage – air drying; using a drying agent or desiccant; and steeping in a glycerine and water solution – are simple and speedy, and produce economical, highly decorative results.

Fresh flowers and leaves must be in prime condition before preserving. When you are picking your own, cut them in the middle of the day when the dew has dried and the flowers have absorbed plenty of water.

Air drying

There are three ways of drying by air: hanging the flowers upside down, standing them upright, or laying them flat on newspaper.

Hanging
This method suits many flowers, especially fairly hardy specimens like sea lavender, statice and love-in-a-mist. Most flowers will be ready in one to three weeks.

1 Bunching Tie the stems together in twos or threes using a piece of string or a rubber band. Hang the bunch upside down in a cool, dry place away from sunlight.

2 Testing dryness Start testing after 1 week. Feel petals gently – they should be dry but not brittle. Stems should dry right up to the flower head. Check regularly – the flowers may take up to 3 weeks to dry out.

Standing upright
Certain tall grasses, seedheads and woody specimens can be left standing in a container to dry. Drying times are the same as for hanging.

Drying upright
Stand a few stems in a container and leave them to dry. Flowers like hydrangea and gypsophila dry better when they start off with a little water in the container. Once this has been absorbed, don't replace it.

Lying flat
Use this method for most grasses, lavender and gourds. Grasses dry in just over a week; gourds take up to three months and are hollow if tapped.

Drying flat Lay the stems flat on a piece of newspaper in a cool, dry place. Spray heavily seeded grasses with hairspray to prevent them from exploding while they are drying.

Method of preserving

This chart lists the most popular plants grown for drying and preserving. It indicates which part of the plant is usually preserved by the most suitable method. (**W** indicates when it is better to start off with water in the container.)

PLANT	WHAT TO PICK	Air – hang	Air – flat	Air – stand	Silica gel	Glycerine
Bay	leaves	✦				
Beech	leaves					✦
Bells of Ireland	flowering stem					✦
Chinese lantern	seedhead	✦		✦		✦
Crocus	opening bud				✦	
Eucalyptus	leaves	✦				
Freesia	full flower				✦	
Globe artichoke	opening/full			✦		
Golden rod	full flower	✦				
Grasses	seedhead		✦	✦		
Gypsophila	full flower			✦(w)	✦	
Honesty	seedhead	✦		✦		
Hydrangea	flower head			✦(w)		✦
Immortelle	full flower	✦				
Ivy	leaves					✦
Larkspur	full flower	✦		✦(w)		
Lavender	opening bud		✦			
Love-in-a-mist	seedhead	✦				
Magnolia	leaves					✦
Marguerite	full flower				✦	
Mimosa	full flower			✦(w)		
Moss	leaves		✦			
Narcissi	full flower				✦	
Oak	leaves					✦
Oats	seedhead			✦		
Onion	seedhead			✦		
Peony	opening bud	✦			✦	
Poppy	seedhead	✦				
Ranunculus	full flower				✦	
Rose	opening bud	✦			✦	
Sea lavender	full flower	✦				
Statice	full flower	✦			✦	
Strawflower	opening bud	✦				
Sunray daisy	full flower	✦				
Teasel	seedhead			✦		
Thistle	flower head			✦		
Violet	full flower				✦	
Wheat	seedhead					✦
Yarrow	flower head	✦		✦		
Zinnia	flower head			✦		

Silica gel

In this drying method, silica gel absorbs moisture from the flower, while preserving its brightness and shape. It is the only way to dry delicate flowers like freesias and narcissi, and is particularly suitable for multi-petalled types like roses and ranunculus.

Silica gel is sold as crystals in craft and hobby stores – buy blue ones that change to pink as they soak up the moisture, so you will know when the flowers are ready. The crystals can be reused – simply warm them in the oven until they have turned blue again.

Airtight method

1 Cutting the flowers Trim the stems off the flowers, leaving a stump about 2cm (¾in) long – once dried you can attach an artificial stem made from florist's wire.

2 Crushing the crystals If the crystals are larger than fine grains of castor sugar, use a coffee grinder to pulverize them – remembering to clean the grinder out thoroughly afterwards – or put them in a strong plastic bag and crush them with a rolling pin.

3 Preparing the container Cover the bottom of an airtight container like a biscuit tin with silica gel crystals. Space the flowers out on top – daisy shapes face down, rounded ones like roses face up. Gently pile more crystals over the flowers, using a tablespoon or sieve, taking care not to crush the petals. If the container is deep enough you can add another layer of flowers. Cover the container with cling film to ensure a good seal, then replace the lid.

4 Checking the flowers Check the flowers at the top of the container every day, shaking off the silica gel very gently. When ready, the petals will feel papery. Take care not to overdry the flowers or they will become brittle.

Microwave method

This way of using silica gel retains the colour and form of the flower well, and takes only minutes to work. Use a container suitable for use in a microwave oven, like an open cardboard box or plastic container without a lid.

Microwaving the plants Prepare the plants as for the *Airtight method*. Place the container of plants and a separate glass of water in the microwave. Set the microwave to full power for 1-4 minutes, depending on the bulk and weight of the flower. Fragile blooms like freesias or narcissi may take only one minute; multi-petalled, cupped varieties take longer. Allow the crystals to cool slightly before testing the dryness of the petals. Repeat if they haven't dried sufficiently.

Glycerine

Preserving woody stemmed foliage or a fleshy plant like bells of Ireland with glycerine gives a waxy quality. Unlike other preserving methods, it doesn't dry the plant. The plant's water is slowly replaced with glycerine which darkens the leaves and stems and keeps them supple and glossy. This takes between one and three weeks, depending on the plant. Glycerine is available from craft and hobby stores and some hardware stores.

1 Picking the foliage Pick the foliage you want to preserve when the leaves are in peak condition.

2 Preparing foliage Remove the lowest leaves from the stems. Cut the stems at an angle, hammering the ends of woody stems to ensure good absorption.

3 Mixing the glycerine Mix a solution of one part glycerine to two parts very hot water, stirring thoroughly.

4 Adding the foliage Stand foliage in a tall, clear container and pour in 7.5cm (3in) of glycerine solution. Put in a cool, dark place for 1-3 weeks, topping up the solution when necessary. If the leaves sweat, wipe with a damp cloth. If they wilt, remove from the solution, cut off the stem ends again, hammer and replace. The foliage is ready when it has changed to a darker colour.

PERFUMED PLEASURES

Potpourri is a wonderful way of adding a subtle hint of fragrance to your home. Not only does it act as a natural air freshener, but its cheerful colours can brighten up a dingy spot too.

Potpourri is a perfumed mixture of dried flowers, herbs, seedheads, spices and essential oils. It has been used for centuries as a natural way of sweetening the air or cloaking less pleasant aromas.

By drying the fresh flowers, you can capture the heady fragrance of summer blooms in potpourri and enjoy their marvellous scent all year round. You may have to refresh the scent after a couple of months with a few drops of essential oils.

In addition to a delicate scent, potpourri brings a welcome splash of colour to a room. The flower petals and seedheads come in natural, rather muted shades as well as more vibrant ones for creating different moods.

Look out for appropriate containers to hold potpourri. A seashell heaped with larkspur petals and lavender heads is just right for a bathroom, while an antique china bowl is charming filled with rose petals in a bedroom. And a wooden bowl packed with spicy, scented pine cones and natural leaves adds a suitably masculine touch in a study.

A bowlful of mixed potpourri fills the room with an explosion of fragrance and adds a touch of vibrant colour.

◀ *Rustic terracotta pots* and dried hydrangeas, poppy heads, roses and seedheads make a logical and decorative accompaniments to dishes of different potpourri.

◩ *Potpourri looks especially lovely* in a ceramic china dish decorated with strawberries and butterflies. It is ideal positioned on a dressing table.

▶ *For a pretty effect,* group four or five blue and white china bowls together and fill each one with potpourri of a different texture and colour.

◩ *Potpourri* needn't always be pink and feminine – maize husks, strips of bark, bay leaves and seedheads would not look out of place in the most masculine setting.

LAVENDER WANDS

Weave scented magic with a length of silky ribbon and a small bunch of fresh lavender – the essential ingredients for a fragrant lavender wand.

This season, preserve the lingering, summery fragrance of fresh lavender by weaving a few stems into a lavender wand. As the lavender dries out, the wand magically releases its pleasing, spicy scent into the room. To perfume a whole room, hang a wand near a window so that the slightest breeze wafts the fragrance around. You can also trap the wand's fragrance inside a drawer or cupboard. All your linen and clothing become delicately scented as well as being protected from moths – lavender is an effective moth repellent.

Lavender gives its name to a soft blue-lilac colour, but the flowers actually vary from deep violet through pink to white. Traditionally, the wands are woven with a ribbon that matches the colour of the lavender, but you may prefer to use a patterned ribbon.

While you can simply buy fresh lavender from a florist, it is much more economical to grow your own. Even if you do not have a garden, a window box or small pot planted with lavender and placed in a sunny spot on a patio gives enough stems for several wands.

In Elizabethan times laundresses were called 'lavendres' as they dried their washing over lavender hedges to make it sweetly scented. Capture the same perfume of lavender in your bedlinen and clothing by placing a lavender wand in a drawer or wardrobe.

MAKING A LAVENDER WAND

For the most aromatic wands, pick the bunch of lavender, and weave the ribbon into it, before the blooms fully unfold. You need an even number of stalks as they are woven in pairs. To make the work as easy as possible, cut the lavender stems as long as you can.

These instructions use narrow ribbon, but using a wider ribbon speeds up the weaving process a little. A double-sided ribbon is the best choice as it has lots of body and gives good coverage. However, a single satin or velvet ribbon is also a good option.

1 Bunching up the lavender Collect together all the lavender into a neat, tightly packed bunch. Make sure that the bottoms of all the flowerheads are at the same level. Wrap the wire firmly round the stems directly underneath the flowerheads.

2 Bending the stems Hold the flowerheads in one hand and bend the stems back over them. Slip an elastic band round the stems, just below flowerheads to hold them in place. Separate stems into pairs, making sure they are straight and evenly spaced around the heads.

3 Starting the weaving Fold one raw end of ribbon back and attach the safety pin through the fold. Insert the safety pin under two stems, pulling the ribbon through to leave a tail of about 50cm (20in). Use the tail to tie a bow at the end of weaving.

TIP
BRITTLE LAVENDER
If the lavender snaps as soon as you try to bend it, it is too dry to work with. You can remedy this by soaking it first in warm water. Immerse stems only until they have softened enough to bend without breaking. Leave it to air dry until it is just damp, then make up the wand.

4 Weaving the ribbon Use the safety pin as a needle to weave ribbon through the pairs of stems, keeping it smooth and flat. Keep the first two rows fairly tight, then slacken off as the shape swells. Weave until you reach the elastic band, then trim the stems to about 12.5cm (5in) from the band. Cut away the band, wrap ribbon firmly round the stems and secure with a knot.

5 Binding the stems Wrap the ribbon diagonally down the stems, twice round the ends of the stems, then back up the stems in the opposite direction. Secure with a knot. Bring the tail of ribbon you left earlier down to join the remaining ribbon. Tie the two together in a knot, then a bow. Use the loop of ribbon formed to hang up the wand.

☑ *Lavender's essential fragrance is concentrated in the tiny calyces surrounding the flowers, but the stalks and leaves are also scented. A wand, where the stems are twisted back to enclose the flower heads, fully exploits the scent.*

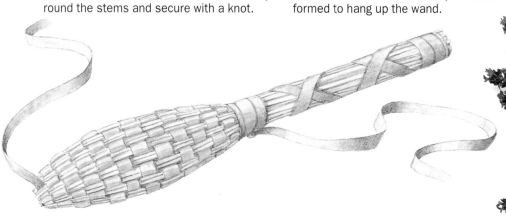

ROSE ARRANGEMENT

With their romantic associations, roses hold a special place in many people's hearts, so what could be more charming than this simple-to-make dried rose arrangement in a terracotta pot?

This arrangement is quick to make and the finished product will grace your window-sill, coffee table or mantelpiece for many months to come. All it takes is a terracotta pot, a ball of dry florists' foam, some soft grey-green sphagnum moss and a few dried roses.

If you have a garden, you can dry your own roses. Alternatively, buy them ready-dried from florists, craft or department stores. The best time to buy dried roses is in the summer or autumn, as this is when the growers dry them. Newly dried roses should have bright flower heads and the leaves should be muted green, not faded grey. Beware of flowers that have been held in stock too long, because they may be brittle.

The sphagnum moss needed for the background to the roses is available from major dried flower suppliers and larger garden centres. Most garden centres and some florists sell terracotta pots. For this display ones which are about 10-15cm (4-6in) tall are ideal.

Although roses are an expensive flower, you do not need very many to create a pleasing effect. The sphagnum moss, which is relatively inexpensive, pads out the arrangement and – with its muted tones of slate green – sets off the roses to perfection.

Beautiful apricot coloured dried roses provide the interest in this easy-to-make arrangement. Why not make a pair of them to display on either side of a mantelpiece?

MAKING THE ARRANGEMENT

It is a good idea to take the terracotta pot along when buying the dried florists' foam to fit in the top. To ensure a truly spherical display choose a ball of foam. Lay the ball on top of the terracotta pot to check that it fits exactly. Make sure that the rim of the pot holds the ball in place at – or just below – its widest point.

Don't underestimate how brittle dried roses are. Be very gentle when pushing them into the florists' foam, otherwise the stems may snap. To avoid this problem make holes in the florists' foam first with a thin skewer or florists' wire. Make sure that the wire is thinner than the rose stem, or the foam won't hold the stem in place.

TIP

DRYING ROSES

To dry your own roses, pick them before they are fully open. Hang them upside down in a dry place, out of direct sunlight. Tie each rose separately by the stem, if possible, to allow the air to circulate around it. Make sure the roses are completely dry before taking them down – the drying times vary, but allow about two weeks.

1 Gluing the base Apply a generous line of adhesive to the inside rim of the terracotta pot. Wait until it becomes tacky and push the ball of florists' foam firmly in place. Leave it to dry.

2 Sticking down the moss Tease a small clump of sphagnum moss from your supply. Apply adhesive to one side of the clump and stick it on to the florists' foam so that it hangs over the rim of the pot to hide the join.

3 Finishing the moss Continue applying sphagnum moss in this way until the florists' foam is covered. If necessary, push short lengths of rose wire bent into a U-shape into the ball to anchor the clumps more securely.

▶ *This variation on the rose-bush theme packs two colours of roses tightly together in concentric circles.*

4 Attaching the first rose Push your skewer into the top of the florists' foam to a depth of about 5cm (2in). Take a dried rose and cut the stem 5cm (2in) from the head at a sharp angle to create a point. Holding the top of the stem carefully, push the rose into the hole made by the skewer. Ease it in until the head nestles against the moss-covered florists' foam.

5 Finishing off Continue inserting the roses at intervals over the foam ball, either at random or following a pattern of circles around the ball. Once all the roses are in place, gently tease out the sphagnum moss so that the roses appear to be deeply bedded in the moss.

BANDS OF COLOUR

*For strikingly handsome and original dried flower arrangements,
you can build up broad, clear-cut, horizontal or concentric bands of floral
colour in containers of any shape.*

Simple, geometric ideas for dried flower displays are especially useful if you are new to flower arranging or have limited time. They are easy to arrange, but the results look highly sophisticated and professional. Indeed, many florist's shops feature costly dried-flower displays based on straightforward bands of colour.

You can base the colour scheme on the room in which the arrangement is to be displayed. Either play up the main colours in your furnishings or take a colour that plays a minor role in the decor and emphasize it in the arrangement. There are no rules about which colours should appear together for these dis-

plays, so you can have fun devising unusual colour schemes. You can combine strongly contrasting colours, put together subtle pastel tones or create monochromatic schemes with bands ranging from dark to pale blue, for example.

Solid blocks of flowers are better for this type of display than an airy silhouette. When you are working on a budget, go for a small but dense display rather than a large, skimpy one. Bear in mind that the smaller the flower, the more you need to group together to make an effective band. In arrangements of concentric circles, the central flowers automatically become the focal point, so choose them with care.

Arranging dried flowers in bands of colour works for any shape or size of display. Here larkspur adds height to the large display of glixia, dahlias, solidaster, roses and caustus lined up below. Rings of moss and roses nestle round achillea in the trug.

A Ring of Roses

Flat or slightly mounded concentric rings of colour in this delightful garden trug (right) look lovely when viewed from above on a low table. An outer ring of reindeer moss and inner rings of rosebuds and fully open miniature roses surround a central mound of delicate achillea. Insert shortened flower stems into a horizontally halved block of dried florists' foam. Arrange the ring of roses first, then fill the centre with achillea. Last of all fix the moss around the edges of the trug with 'hairpins' of thin wire.

A Striped Basket Arrangement

In this multicoloured display (below) a block of dried florists' foam is cut to fit the basket and impaled on a florists' prong fixed to the bottom of the basket with mastic. Cut the flower stems short and work from the central stripe of blue globe thistles outwards.

Insert the blooms – pink and creamy helichrysums and orange carthamus – in straight rows, one flower wide. As an unusual finishing touch, you can add lengths of straw between the rows. Make sure you cut these to the same length before inserting them.

A Tiered Display

Displays of tiered bands of horizontal colour look best viewed from the front, on a table, mantelpiece or shelf. This tiered display (left) is easy to make, but is more expensive because of its size – for a more economical version, you could make a smaller display with just the lower two or three tiers. Start arranging the flowers from the back and work forwards. Insert larkspur into a block of dried florists' foam, which is firmly fixed to the bottom of the basket. To get the fanned effect of this display, continue adding the flowers – glixia, dahlias and yellow solidaster – in progressively shorter rows. Finally add a mixture of roses and green caustus along the front.

A Dried Flower Swag

Bright coloured swags of dried flowers and foliage make natural, country style decorations for a special occasion. Made in colours to coordinate with your room, a swag gives a lovely year-long display.

T raditionally, decorative swags are made of berries and evergreen leaves to hang across the fireplace at Christmas. By using dried flowers and foliage, you can make a pretty, fragrant swag at any time of the year which will last for months.

Swags can be made to any length for hanging horizontally or vertically. The one illustrated here is 75cm (30in) long, just long enough to drape into a shallow curve. A dried flower swag looks really effective in a country style kitchen, arranged across a cupboard door or the top of a kitchen dresser. Formal hallways will look warm and welcoming with a pretty swag hanging over an alcove, draped over a balustrade or above a doorway. Or simply display your swag across the chimney breast or around a picture in your living room.

Florists and craft stores usually stock a good selection of dried flowers, or you can dry your own. When choosing dried flowers and foliage for your swag, make sure you include large and small blooms with a variety of textures, shapes, scents and colours. An assortment gives depth and interest to the arrangement as well as making it look natural.

As decorative as fresh flowers, these dried ones add a country touch to last the whole year round. Pretty bows in coordinating colours disguise hanging loops at either end.

MAKING A FLOWER SWAG

YOU WILL NEED

❖ A selection of DRIED FLOWERS

❖ Medium gauge FLORIST'S WIRE

❖ SCISSORS

❖ RAFFIA

❖ REEL WIRE

❖ RIBBON

This swag is made up of dried helichrysum, lavender, roses, marjoram, nigella, larkspur, hydrangea and eucalyptus leaves tied on to a base of raffia. You can experiment with any dried flowers and foliage that have firm stems.

If you're going to hang your swag against a flat surface such as a wall, cupboard or mirror, you should put more flowers towards the front and fill up the back with bunches of foliage. However if the swag is to be seen from all sides, make sure the flowers and foliage are evenly distributed around it. Experiment with the arrangement of each bunch as you position it, until you are happy with the effect.

1 Wiring bunches together Cut 7.5cm (3in) lengths of florist's wire. Trim flower and foliage stems to 10-15cm (4-6in) lengths. For each cluster, gather together three to six stems of roughly the same mix of flowers and foliage. Wind wire firmly round the stems, leaving about 2.5cm (1in) of the stems below the wire.

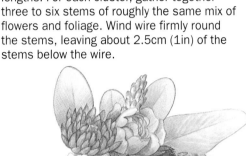

2 Making hanging loops Cut a bundle of raffia to about 75cm (30in). Bend two 10cm (4in) pieces of florist's wire into loops. To hang the swag, bind one loop firmly to each end of the raffia with reel wire. Tie off the end of the wire securely before cutting it.

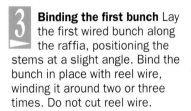

3 Binding the first bunch Lay the first wired bunch along the raffia, positioning the stems at a slight angle. Bind the bunch in place with reel wire, winding it around two or three times. Do not cut reel wire.

4 Adding the bunches Place the second bunch at a different angle to the first, but close enough to cover the first stems. Bind it as before. Repeat with the remaining bunches, distributing the colours and flower shapes evenly.

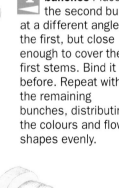

5 Covering the ends When the swag is complete, finish with a round headed bunch, cutting the stems shorter than the others, if necessary. Tie ribbon bows over the ends to cover the reel wire binding the loops and any protruding stems.

T I P

FLOWER FOCUS

Make scarcer, more expensive flowers a focal point by grouping them together at the centre of the swag. Position any remaining expensive blooms at each end of the swag.

To position the swag, first check the fixing points by draping a 75cm (30in) tape measure where you want the swag to hang. Then fix two small picture hooks securely in the wall and hitch the hanging loops over them.

DRIED FLOWER MIRROR

Decorate a plain mirror frame with dried flowers and moss to give it an attractive new appearance. Easy to create and pretty to look at, the mirror adds an original charm to any room scheme.

A decorative mirror hung above a fireplace or taking centre stage on a wall can be just as handsome a feature as a picture. Beautifully framed mirrors are usually quite an investment. However, if you use dried flowers to dress up a plain frame, you don't have to spend a fortune to produce an eyecatching focal point for your room.

Beneath the trimmings on this mirror lies an ordinary, inexpensive pine frame – one of many in all shapes and sizes that you can buy from your local department or furniture store. The use of dried flowers is as economical as possible, too. Most of the frame is covered with a layer of flat moss with some well chosen blooms at the corners to add interest and catch the eye. Bushy hydrangea heads are particularly good value for money as one covers a whole corner. Then it's up to you how many other flowerheads you insert to add extra colour and shape to the mirror.

Red, purple and green make up the colour scheme here, but you can choose alternative colours and flowers to coordinate with your room's decorating scheme. An accent colour from your curtains or other soft furnishings is a good starting point for a colour theme for the mirror surround. You have the entire range of dried flowers at your disposal – from bright yellow sunflowers or African daisies to blue lavender, orange golden rod, peachy pink and apricot roses or any number of dyed flowers.

This charming dried flower mirror, hung in pride of place above the mantelpiece, is set off by coloured candles flanking it on each side.

COVERING THE FRAME

All you need to cover the mirror surround is some flat moss, dried flowers, stub wire and a glue gun. You can use a tube of strong, quick-drying adhesive instead, but a glue gun is less messy and is definitely quicker. A hot glue gun is inexpensive and available from any DIY store.

YOU WILL NEED

- ❖ RECTANGULAR MIRROR 30 x 40cm (12 x 15¾in)
- ❖ FLAT MOSS (BLANKET MOSS)
- ❖ 4 HYDRANGEA HEADS
- ❖ 3 BUNCHES OF AGERATUM
- ❖ 32 RED ROSES
- ❖ FINE STUB WIRE
- ❖ HOT GLUE GUN
- ❖ SMALL PAIR OF SCISSORS

1 Attaching the moss
Trim lengths of flat moss to 6mm (¼in) more than the width of the mirror frame. Using the glue gun, apply glue to the back of the first piece of moss and press into position. Continue sticking on the moss until the entire frame is covered, being careful not to leave any unsightly gaps.

2 Attaching the hydrangeas
Take a hydrangea head and glue it in place at the top left-hand corner of the frame. Press the head into place firmly, taking care to space out the petals so that it covers the corner well. Repeat for the remaining three corners.

3 Attaching the ageratum
Arrange four or five stems of the ageratum and bind them together towards the top of the stems with a length of fine stub wire. Trim the stems to about 3cm (1¼in) below the stub wire. Continue wiring up the ageratum until you have about six small bunches for each corner of the mirror. Glue these in place on either side of the hydrangea heads.

4 Opening the roses
Briefly hold each rose over the spout of a boiling kettle to steam them. As the petals become damp with steam, ease the outer petals open, leaving the centre of the rose intact.

5 Attaching the roses
Carefully break the stems off all the roses. Apply glue to the bottom of the rose heads and press them in place throughout the flower clumps at each corner. Position the roses to cover any gaps and hide the ageratum stems from view.

6 Finishing off Hang the mirror in place and check for gaps, adding extra flowers or moss where necessary. Trim any wisps of moss with small scissors.

The dried ingredients for this mirror surround are — from right to left — ageratum, flat moss, hydrangea heads and roses.

DRIED FLOWER BASKET

A pretty basket of informally arranged dried flowers creates a cheerful, long-lasting display and is an easy way to bring a splash of country colour and charm into your home.

One of the pleasures of dried flower arrangements is that unlike displays of fresh flowers, they can last for many months, and even longer if you look after them. So taking time with the choice and arrangement of flowers is well worth the effort.

The principles of working with dried flowers are similar to making formal fresh flower displays – and no more difficult. All you need is a suitable container such as a basket, and some florists' foam (oasis), which is readily available from florists and garden centres. When buying the florists' foam, make sure that you choose the right type. Dried flower foam is brown or grey and fairly rigid; the foam for fresh arrangements is green and softer, and is designed to absorb and hold water.

Place the florists' foam in the bottom of the container and arrange the flowers by inserting the stems into it. You often need to wire several flower stems together, to strengthen them and make them last longer. Step-by-step instructions for making this display are given over the page.

The yellow and orange flowers used in the display above combine to create a glorious burst of golden colour. Helichrysums are mixed with orange nipplewort, marigolds, zinnias, carthamus in natural orange and dyed bronze, sunflowers and small chrysanthemums.

The rich textures and colours of these dried flowers filling this basket is bound to attract attention wherever it's displayed. A hall table or an empty fireplace are particularly suitable spots.

47

BASKET BONANZA

Baskets make ideal containers for dried flowers as the natural tones of the wicker are the perfect foil for the subtle colouring of many dried flowers. Choose a rounded, roughly woven basket to create a country-cottage look – one with a central handle is easy to move.

Before you buy the dried flowers, decide on the main colour scheme and the size and variety of flowerheads that you need. If you are using a small basket, weigh it down with pebbles to stop it toppling over as you arrange the flower sprays.

In arrangements such as this one, you should group smaller flowers together to give the display touches of solid colour. With larger flowerheads such as sunflowers, it is often best to insert them individually, as each one of the imposing, yellow heads provides plenty of impact within the display. If the other flowers are closely packed together they help support the weight of the larger, heavier flowerheads. To create even stronger patches of colour, try wiring two or three larger flowers together.

YOU WILL NEED
❖ DRY FLORISTS' FOAM
❖ WICKER BASKET
❖ SHARP KNIFE
❖ STUB WIRE
❖ ORANGE NIPPLEWORT
❖ CARTHAMUS
❖ ZINNIAS
❖ MARIGOLDS
❖ HELICHRYSUMS
❖ SMALL CHRYSANTHEMUMS
❖ SMALL SUNFLOWERS

▲ *The scene-stealing dried flower display shown on the previous page is made up from a selection of (from top to bottom) nipplewort, chrysanthemum, zinnia, helichrysum, marigold and carthamus. You can also use sunflowers if any are available.*

1 Shaping the foam Press the base of the basket on to the foam block so it leaves an imprint, then cut round the imprint with a sharp knife. If the sides of the basket slope, cut the foam at an angle to fit.

2 Wiring the flowers Cut the flower stems to roughly the same length. Put the chrysanthemums and nipplewort into separate small groups. Wrap the stems of these smaller flowers with stub wire, securing in small sprays.

3 Shaping the display Insert the nipplewort into the foam at regular intervals, pressing the stems further into the foam nearer the edge to create a rounded shape. Add sprays of chrysanthemums and carthamus into the gaps, distributing them evenly.

4 Filling in Insert zinnias, marigolds, helichrysums and sunflowers, turning the basket as you work to achieve a round, even shape.

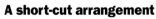

TIP

KEEPING UP APPEARANCES
To keep your display of dried flowers looking at its best, try dusting it very lightly with a feather duster or gently blowing over it with a cool hairdryer.

A short-cut arrangement

For an orderly display in a smaller basket, a symmetrical arrangement looks very effective. To make the display shown here, fit the foam into the basket as shown in step 1 above, then insert a neat row of yellow chrysanthemums round the edge. Fill in the centre of the basket with wired sprays of helichrysums in orange and apricot colours.

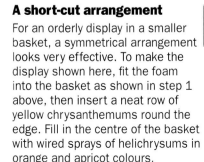

DRIED FLOWER WALL DISPLAY

Spice up a blank kitchen or dining room wall with this unusual dried flower arrangement, featuring cinnamon sticks and dried and varnished miniature bread rolls.

Wall-hung flower arrangements have much to commend them. They leave horizontal surfaces clutter free, require half the material of a similar sized all-round display to achieve the same impact and are protected from accidental damage. Delicate dried flowers especially benefit from such protection and, as they don't need watering or frequent renewal, you can position them high up on a wall without causing inconvenience.

This arrangement includes some dyed dried flowers, but you can stick to natural tones. Alternatively, include a few silk flowers, perhaps with a seasonal reference, and change them from time to time. Bundles of cinnamon sticks and tiny bread rolls add an unusual touch. Buy the rolls ready wired and varnished from florists or make your own. If you like, you can substitute wired heads of garlic or dried chilli peppers for an artistic, culinary alternative.

A terracotta container, with warm, earthy tones, is used for this display, but you can just as easily use a wicker, bamboo, glazed ceramic or china container. As no watering is involved, a moss-lined wall-hung basket or wirework half-basket is a good option. These are readily available from garden centres. Try to avoid ornate containers, as dried flowers are themselves richly intricate and detailed.

A homey culinary touch, in the form of cinnamon sticks and varnished bread rolls, adds character to a generously full, informal dried flower display in a terracotta wall vase.

MAKING THE DISPLAY

This arrangement is made with crumpled wire-mesh netting, which is used to anchor the stems of the flowers firmly in place. If you want, you can pack the container with large chunks of dried florists' foam instead, as this works just as well. Cover your work area with a polythene sheet or newspaper to catch dried flower fragments which break off as you work.

YOU WILL NEED

- ❖ WALL-HUNG TERRACOTTA CONTAINER, 25cm (10in) in diameter
- ❖ WATER-BASED PAINT, (optional)
- ❖ WIRE-MESH NETTING
- ❖ SECATEURS

Dried flowers:
- ❖ CARTHAMUS, one bunch
- ❖ TANSY, one bunch
- ❖ CORNFLOWERS, one bunch
- ❖ BLEACHED GYPSOPHILA, one bunch
- ❖ WOOD DAISIES, one bunch
- ❖ CREAM ROSES, one bunch
- ❖ RED-DYED ACHILLEA, one bunch
- ❖ STRAWFLOWERS, five wired stems
- ❖ TEN CINNAMON STICKS
- ❖ FINE FLORISTS' WIRE
- ❖ TWO MINIATURE BREAD ROLLS

1 Preparing the container If necessary, sponge a new container with water-based paint to soften its colour. When dry, pack tightly with crumpled wire-mesh netting.

2 Establishing the height Cut the stems of a bunch of carthamus and tansy to 35cm (14in) in length. Build up the back row with stems of carthamus on one side and tansy on the other, so they overlap each other and are angled outwards slightly from an imaginary centre point.

3 Building up density Cut the cornflower, gypsophila, wood daisy and remaining carthamus and tansy stems to varying heights, from 17-27cm (7-11in). Working from back to front and from tall to short, fill in the centre of the display with small bunches of each type. Keep some of the tansy and gypsophila to add later on. Angle the stems outwards so that the display's width is roughly one and a half times the width of the container.

4 Adding the focal points Insert a cluster of roses on one side and a small cluster of strawflowers around them. Tie two groups of 4-5 cinnamon sticks in bundles with florists' wire. Insert one bundle between the roses and strawflowers and the other low down towards the centre. Insert two miniature bread rolls towards the front of the display.

5 Filling in the foreground Cut the red achillea stems to varying lengths, ranging from 12-17cm (5-7in). Insert them at the front of the display, with some stems resting on the rim. Finally, insert individual tansy and gypsophila stems, angled outwards and downwards, to overhang and soften the line of the rim.

DECORATIVE ROLLS

You can make your own bread rolls for decorative purposes. Use a basic bread or pizza dough mix, making sure the mixture is fairly stiff. Mould into sausage shapes and plait for the loaf or twist into knots for cottage loaf styles. Sprinkle with poppy or caraway seeds and bake in a hot oven till they sound hollow when tapped. Leave to cool, then pierce with florists' wire and twist wire ends to form a stem. Leave to harden for two days, then glaze with two coats of clear varnish.

▼ *From top to bottom, the ingredients used in the display shown here are cornflower, wood daisy, strawflower, gypsophila, carthamus, dyed achillea, rose and tansy.*

WILLOW RINGS

*Enhance the natural beauty of a willow ring, with its
intertwining stems and rich brown colouring, by trimming
it with a few, well-chosen dried flowers.*

S trategically placed above a fireplace, nestled on a dresser or enlivening a plain expanse of wall, a trimmed willow wreath is sure to become a focal point in a room. The wreath itself is lovely and, trimmed with clusters of dried flowers and foliage, it becomes an unusual and special dried flower decoration.

The earthy tones of the willow ring are a perfect foil for a golden autumn palette of flowerheads, leaves and ears of wheat. However, there is no reason why you shouldn't select material in the colour of your choice, using a range of tones of a single colour or a mixed medley of many lively shades. As a rule, several sizes of flowerheads make a better display – the larger blooms give it shape and form.

Although the result here looks extremely professional, the ring is simple to decorate. Using florists' foam to anchor the flowers to the ring means that you don't have to spend time wiring individual blooms to the willow. It also allows you to experiment with the positioning of the flowers. If they don't look quite right first time, you can simply pull them out and push them into the foam in another place or at a different angle.

The yellows, cream and green of the sunflowers, roses, anaphalis and millet work well together. As an added bonus, the anaphalis has a delicate, chamomile-like scent that gently perfumes the air.

ATTACHING THE DRIED FLOWERS

YOU WILL NEED

- ❖ WILLOW RING
- ❖ BLOCK OF DRIED FLORISTS' FOAM
- ❖ KNIFE
- ❖ FLORISTS' TAPE
- ❖ MEDIUM STUB WIRE
- ❖ BUNCH OF ITALIAN MILLET
- ❖ 6 SUNFLOWERS
- ❖ 20 YELLOW ROSES
- ❖ 6 BUNCHES OF ANAPHALIS
- ❖ BUNCH OF LAVENDER

This display is based on a 35cm (13¾in) diameter ring and is trimmed with three clusters of flowers, set at regular intervals. Insert the different ingredients one at a time to build up each cluster.

1 Attaching the foam Cut three wedges, 5cm (2in) thick, from the block of foam. Place the first wedge at the top of the ring, with the other two spaced at equal intervals around it. Secure them with florists' tape, wrapping it tightly round both the foam wedges and the ring.

2 Inserting the millet Push the stems of millet into the foam at different angles to set the shape and span of the arrangement. To add interest, push some stems in further than others to make them different lengths. Make sure that the longer lengths follow round the curve of the willow ring.

3 Adding the sunflowers Cut the stems of the dried sunflowers so they are about 7.5cm (3in) long. Push the first stem into the top left hand corner of one of the pieces of foam. Position the next sunflower towards the bottom right hand corner. Repeat for the other pieces of foam.

4 Adding the roses Cut the stems of the roses so that they are about 5cm (2in) long. Holding each flower firmly between your fingers – at the top of the stem to avoid crushing the petals – push the roses into the foam. Arrange two groups of three roses in each block of foam.

◣ *A close-up of the posies on the willow ring shows the position of the flowers clearly and how the millet follows the curve of the ring.*

5 Adding the anaphalis Wire up small bunches of anaphalis and push them into the foam between the groups of roses and the sunflowers, so that each block of foam has three or four bunches.

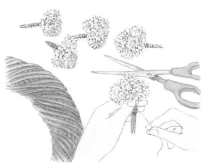

VARIATION ON THE THEME

If you don't have the time to make the arrangement shown above, or prefer something less elaborate, you can use the same method on a smaller, simpler scale.

To arrange the ring shown on the right, attach one block of foam at the top of a 30cm (12in) diameter ring and stud it with a spray of roses, marigolds, achillea and stalks of wheat. In this case, the ring is made of twisted vine stems rather than willow as above.

6 Finishing off Add stems of lavender in groups of three or four, following the line of the millet. Then push four or five stems into the centre of each block of foam to add extra colour. Fill in any gaps that remain with sunflower or rose leaves. To hang the ring up, just thread a short length of string through the back of the ring, directly behind one of the blocks of foam.

SEEDHEADS AND GRASSES

Capture the sun-washed summer colour of hedgerows and meadows with this informal display of dried grasses, seedheads and flowers, set in a simple earthenware vase.

Mixing wild flowers with cultivated ones always adds informal, country-fresh charm to an arrangement. In terms of economy, a selection of wild flowers, seedheads and grasses can bulk out a display for virtually no extra cost and, if dried, they can be re-used for months on end.

You can collect wild flowers, seedheads and grasses from roadsides, hedgerows and wasteland, but try to stick to obviously common and widespread species, such as cow parsley, teasel, rose-bay willowherb, burdock, mullein, foxglove, dock, ground elder, traveller's joy and wild clematis. Never uproot a wild plant, col-

lect all the flowers or seedheads from a group of plants or take any part of a plant that is an endangered species – you can get lists of plants protected by law from local authorities and libraries. Technically, you need permission from the landowner before picking permitted wild flowers, and you should never pick flowers or foliage when in a state or national park or nature reserve.

You can grow wild flowers, grasses and seedheads from seed. Meadow, field and woodland mixtures are available to suit both sunny and shady spots. Some garden centres sell young wild flower plants in containers.

This informal display of dried, wild and cultivated flowers, seedheads and grasses has the unpretentious, slightly random charm of a just-picked bunch of flowers.

MAKING THE ARRANGEMENT

Although specific ingredients are listed, you can use almost any similar coloured dried material, as long as you have a good contrast of form, size and texture. The effect you want to create with the finished display is one of a hand-picked bunch, simply lowered into a vase.

◨ *This arrangement has a natural look, but you can add dyed ingredients for a spot of colour if you like.*

1 Establishing the height Set the height of the display – roughly twice the height of the container – using the tallest grasses and bulrushes. Place the highest material towards the back, with shorter material in front. Leave the stems to settle naturally, establishing the width of the display.

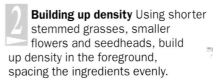

▶ *From top to bottom: canary grass, bulrush, teasel, achillea, sunflower, helipterum, poppy, reed grass, wood flower, gypsophila.*

2 Building up density Using shorter stemmed grasses, smaller flowers and seedheads, build up density in the foreground, spacing the ingredients evenly.

3 Creating focal points Varying the stem heights, incorporate larger flowers and seedheads, such as teasel, sunflower and achillea, into the display. Position the lowest focal point on an imaginary centre line, running vertically through the display.

WILD ALTERNATIVES

The following wild flowers, grasses and seedheads are all easily found or grown and make delightful ingredients for a wild flower display:

Burdock	Hop
Campion	Knapweed
Common flax	Loosestrife
Cornflower	Mayweed
Dock	Milfoil
Evening primrose	Mugwort
Fleabane	Mullein
Foxglove	Nipplewort
Goldenrod	Ox-eye daisy
Ground elder	Plantain
Heather	Poppy
Hempnettle	Rape

DRIED FLOWER CONE

*An eye-catching conical display of dried flowers
is simple to make and forms a stylish and long-lasting decoration
that can take pride of place in any room.*

The secret behind this dramatic dried-flower arrangement is its ingenious cone-shaped support made from chicken wire and florists' foam. Once you've made the framework, arranging the flowers is easy, as all you need to do is push them up against the wire so they are held securely in place.

As only the outside of the support is covered with dried flowers, you don't need lots of blooms to create an abundant looking display. It's important not to skimp on the dried flowers, though, as the success of the arrangement relies on a densely packed look that covers all the wire netting beneath. It is best to opt for large-headed varieties such as achillea, as they fill the wire frame quickly and economically. Flowers with straight, sturdy stems are easier to push into the foam, so avoid wispy grasses or very small flowers.

A plain container sets off the display well. It needs to be quite substantial, otherwise the finished cone may be top heavy. Alternatively, weight the base of a vase with a few stones. The glossy green ceramic jar used above is ideal, or you can substitute a classic terracotta flowerpot for a more rustic feel.

Subtly coloured dried flowers in soft bluey greens, dusky mauves and greenish greys are highlighted with a few carefully placed cream roses in this dried flower cone. Whether placed as a focal point on a coffee table or to add interest in the corner of a room, it makes an excellent year-round arrangement.

MAKING THE DISPLAY

The dried flowers used here are readily available from most craft stores. They are usually sold in bunches. As a rough guide, this display uses two bunches of each type of dried flower.

When you are inserting the dried flowers into the wire and foam frame of the cone make sure you achieve a good balance of colours by spreading the different ingredients evenly throughout the display. The easiest way to do this is to start at the base of the cone, using a mixture of flowers, and then to work your way up to the top in a spiral fashion.

From top to bottom, the dried flowers used in this arrangement are mauve achillea, poppy seedhead, purple nipplewort, echinops, Nigella orientalis, mauve amaranthus, rose, eucalyptus leaves, blue amaranthus, green/grey achillea.

YOU WILL NEED

- ❖ VASE, 28cm (11in) in diameter
- ❖ PAIR OF COMPASSES
- ❖ THIN CARDBOARD
- ❖ MASKING TAPE
- ❖ MEDIUM-MESH CHICKEN WIRE
- ❖ WIRE CUTTERS
- ❖ PROTECTIVE GLOVES
- ❖ DRIED FLORISTS' FOAM
- ❖ DYED OR NATURAL EUCALYPTUS LEAVES
- ❖ ECHINOPS
- ❖ DYED MAUVE ACHILLEA
- ❖ DYED GREEN/GREY ACHILLEA
- ❖ POPPY SEEDHEADS
- ❖ DYED MAUVE AMARANTHUS
- ❖ DYED BLUE AMARANTHUS
- ❖ DYED PURPLE NIPPLEWORT
- ❖ *NIGELLA ORIENTALIS*
- ❖ CREAM ROSES

1 Making the template Using a pair of compasses, draw a semicircle with a radius of 35cm (14in) on to a piece of cardboard and cut it out. Roll it into a cone and push the wide end into the vase to check the fit, then secure it with masking tape. Take the cone out of the vase and, using a pencil, draw a line down the side of the cone where the edges overlap. Peel off the tape, unroll the cone and cut along the marked line.

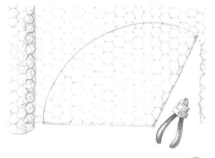

2 Making the wire cone Lay the template flat and place the chicken wire on top. Wear gloves and use the wire cutters to cut out the wire, following the edges of the cardboard as a guide. Roll the wire into a cone and twist the loose bits of wire over one another to hold it in place. Pack the cone with pieces of florists' foam.

3 Preparing the base Put several stones in the base of the vase to weigh it down and pack the rest with pieces of florists' foam. Push the base of the wire cone into the vase and use tape to secure it firmly in place. This will be concealed by the flowers.

4 Arranging the display Trim the flower stems so they are about 10cm (4in) long. Lay them out in groups. Ignoring the cream roses, push a mix-and-match selection of the remaining flowers into the wire, starting at the base and spiralling upwards. Spread them out evenly, keeping an eye on the overall shape. If necessary, trim the stems further.

5 Finishing off Carefully insert the cream roses at equal intervals around the cone. Make any final adjustments by moving or adding flowers until you are satisfied with the appearance.

The exotic look of golden oak leaves combined with rich red orchids and Hypericum berries, makes a special table-top display for a festive occasion. The leaves gleam in the subtle, mood-setting glow of candlelight.

THE MIDAS TOUCH

Gilded leaves – real or silk leaves simply sprayed with gold paint – lend a theatrical touch to many items around the home. Use them to add glamour and glitz to floral displays, table settings or plain ornaments.

Take one can of gold spray paint, some real leaves from your garden and turn everyday items into decorative treasures. Sturdy fresh or dried leaves with well-defined shapes, such as ivy, holly, oak or eucalyptus, take the paint well and last for weeks. For more permanent effects, coat artificial leaves made from silk, paper or plastic with the paint – again choose leaves with strong shapes for the best results.

To spray the leaves, lay them on a sheet of newspaper. Work outside – spray paint has a tendency to drift so you may find you coat more than bargained for if you don't take sensible precau-

tions. Spray lots of leaves at once, coating them all on one side first, then the other.

One of the most effective ideas is to intersperse gold-sprayed leaves among fresh floral arrangements – they add unexpected drama to a display, especially in candlelight. Twist stems of gold sprayed ivy round candlesticks for an instant festive makeover. Gold-sprayed leaves also look fabulous trimming the edge of a plain picture or mirror frame, recreating the look of an expensive gilded frame for next to nothing. Glue the gold-coated leaves in place, overlapping them for total coverage.

◀ **Ivy leaves take gold** paint particularly well. Mix the occasional sprayed leaf with fresh, unsprayed leaves to create a simple yet effective bed on which to present fresh fruit or nuts during the festive season.

▶ **Gold-paper leaves**, usually reserved for cake-decorating, find a new purpose tied to the stems of wine glasses. Trimmed this way the glasses, laid out for a buffet, set an instant and memorable party mood.

◀ **Oak leaves**, generously coated with gold paint, hide a damaged mirror frame. Use the leaves liberally, overlapping them and letting the edges lift to suggest the fragility and three-dimensional look of an antique gilded frame.

▶ **Conical trees** made from dried, golden leaves are an unusual, miniature alternative to a traditional Christmas tree. Make the trees by embedding the leaves into a base of dried-flower florists' foam mounted on a branch set into a terracotta pot – in the same way as you would make a dried flower pomander tree.

FESTIVE NUT BOUQUET

This gilded everlasting bouquet is ideal as a centrepiece for special occasion meals: make it well in advance to leave you free to relax and enjoy family and friends during the festive season.

F lower arrangements and festive occasions go hand in hand, but arranging and caring for fresh flowers can be time-consuming – an important factor when you have special meals to prepare and people to entertain. This burnished bouquet of gilded walnut flowers with petals of glycerine-preserved leaves perfectly captures the spirit of Christmas but needs no looking after once it's made. When the season ends, simply wrap the bouquet in tissue paper and store in a box for next year.

Unlike fresh flowers, which rocket in price when demand is high, the cost of this sophisticated arrangement is modest. It's worth making more than one, for a grouped display or to give as gifts.

Make sure the walnuts are fresh, to ensure that you can wire them up easily, and that they are dry and clean before gilding. You can use bronze, silver or copper gilt, or a mixture, as well as gold. Although gilt cream is used, you could use gilt spray paint instead for a slightly less glossy effect. For a luxurious sheen, apply a coat of gilt varnish once the gilt cream has dried. Gilt cream and varnish are available from art shops.

Glycerine-preserved leaves can be hard to come by commercially but it's easy to prepare them yourself. Cut 30-45cm (12-18in) branches of healthy oak or beech leaves in late summer, before they begin to change colour. Place in a tall, thin container filled with a mixture of half glycerine, half hot water, topping up as the mixture is absorbed. Fully preserved leaves turn a rich brown, with a leathery, flexible texture.

Set in a golden pot, walnuts burnished with gilt cream and decorated with preserved leaves add a sparkle of sophistication to a festive table.

MAKING THE DISPLAY

No quantities are given for the nuts, as terracotta flowerpots and florists' foam balls vary enormously in size. Choose a ball that is slightly wider than the diameter of the flowerpot rim. Walnuts are cheap enough to buy more than you need – you can always serve the surplus with cheese at the end of a meal.

YOU WILL NEED

- ❖ TERRACOTTA FLOWERPOT
- ❖ JAR OF GILT CREAM
- ❖ SOFT CLOTH or SMALL PAINT BRUSH
- ❖ JAR OF GILT VARNISH (optional)
- ❖ GLYCERINED LEAVES
- ❖ GLUE GUN and GLUE STICKS or MULTI-PURPOSE GLUE
- ❖ DRIED-FLOWER FLORISTS' FOAM BALL
- ❖ FRESH WALNUTS
- ❖ WIRE CUTTERS
- ❖ MEDIUM-GAUGE FLORISTS' STUB WIRES

1 Preparing the pot Use a soft cloth to apply the gilt cream to the outside and the inner rim of a clean, dry terracotta pot. The effect can be slightly uneven. Leave to dry. Apply a thin coat of gilt varnish in the same way, if wished, and leave to dry for several hours.

2 Adding leaves Select four to six similar sized leaves. One at a time, apply glue to their undersides and press firmly and neatly round the rim, stalk-end up, spacing them evenly apart and slightly overlapping the rim. Gently bend the leaves over the rim, and press to adhere. Make sure they stick.

3 Fixing the foam base Run a band of glue around the edge and inside of the pot rim. Press the florists' foam ball firmly on to the flowerpot, holding it in place for a few minutes to ensure good contact with the glue.

4 Preparing the walnuts Gild the walnuts as above and leave to dry; apply gilt varnish, if wished, and let dry. Use wire cutters to snip the stub wire into 5cm (2in) lengths. Then push a wire gently but firmly into each walnut, where the two halves join at the base.

◩ *The golden nutty centrepiece is simple to make using gilt cream — and varnish for an extra glow, if desired — available from most art shops. Choose oak or beech leaves to preserve for the flower petals.*

5 Making the flowers To make the petals, glue along the central vein of a leaf then wrap it round a walnut, leaving the top and wired base free. If the leaves are small, you may need two to achieve a generously full effect; if they are large, trim them down to size. Continue until all the walnuts are wrapped.

TIP
CHOOSING GLUES

A glue gun releases melted hot glue under pressure, and bonding is instant; it's useful if you do a lot of craftwork but is costly and needs careful handling – ideally with protective gloves – as the glue gets very hot. Multi-purpose glue takes longer to dry but is cheaper and widely available.

6 Making the bouquet Before gluing, test how many walnuts fit round the top of the ball – ideally, they should be as close together as possible. Squeeze a blob of glue on to a walnut where the wire protrudes from its base. Starting from the rim, push the wire firmly into the foam ball. Complete the bottom row, then work upwards. Turn the display as you proceed, to ensure that the ball is completely covered.

GOLDEN CHRISTMAS BASKET

*Using shimmering gold as an accent colour, turn a basket
of dried flowers, cones and seedheads into a festive ornament, perfect
for use as a Christmas decoration.*

A dd the Midas touch to a seasonal dried flower arrangement by spraying it with gold paint. Sturdy materials, such as small fir cones and poppy seedheads, are ideal for this sumptuous gilded effect. Balance them with fragile, coloured hydrangeas, whose natural pastel hues will show through the gilding to add a subtle shimmer. Complete the display with some glittering highlights in the form of gold Christmas tree baubles, which will pick up the gold accents, catch the light and create sparkling reflections.

Use spray paint to colour the plant material – it gives quick results, and it's easy to control the amount of paint you apply. There is a range of gold spray paints from which to choose – from mellow, old-gold shades to bright, brassy hues. Make sure that you buy a shade of gold to suit your taste and the room. Some shops have tester pots available, so you can check the colour before you buy. If you take a spare seedhead or fir cone with you, you can test the colour exactly.

The arrangement is designed to look attractive from all angles – taking pride of place on an occasional table, perhaps – but it looks just as effective set against a wall, on a mantelpiece or sitting on a windowsill.

The muted colours of this display show through a shimmering coat of gold. With any leftover gold paint, you can spray a couple of dried artichokes; they create a good visual link when placed by the dried-flower basket.

MAKING THE ARRANGEMENT

1 Cutting the foam Use a sharp knife to cut the foam so that it fits neatly into the basket. Place the cut-off sections on the top to create a domed shape, and anchor them in place with lengths of stub wire.

2 Wiring the fir cones Wrap a length of stub wire around the base of a fir cone to hold it firmly. Straighten the end to form a stem about 10cm (4in) long. Push the stem into the foam. Repeat for the other fir cones, positioning them at irregular intervals around the basket.

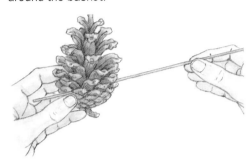

YOU WILL NEED

- ❖ RECTANGULAR BASKET with handle
- ❖ BLOCK OF DRIED FLORISTS' FOAM
- ❖ SHARP KNIFE, SCISSORS
- ❖ STUB WIRE
- ❖ FIVE DRIED HYDRANGEA HEADS
- ❖ SIX FIR CONES
- ❖ SIXTEEN POPPY SEEDHEADS
- ❖ TWELVE DRIED RED ROSES
- ❖ SMALL GOLD BAUBLES
- ❖ GOLD SPRAY PAINT
- ❖ NEWSPAPER

3 Attaching more plant material Wire the hydrangea heads as in step 2 and space them evenly around the foam, so that they cover most of the area. Cut the stems of the poppy seedheads down to about 10cm (4in) and insert them into the arrangement at intervals.

4 Adding the roses Carefully cut the stems of the roses into points about 10cm (4in) below the head. Push them into the foam at intervals, making sure you fill any spaces left in the arrangement.

5 Spray-painting Work outside or in a well-ventilated room and wear rubber gloves. Lay the arrangement on newspaper. Spray it lightly with gold paint, covering both the ingredients and the basket evenly. Leave it to dry. Respray it for a deeper colour if necessary.

T I P

TWO TONE ARRANGEMENT

For an alternative arrangement that adds depth and colour to the gold-sprayed dried flowers and seedheads, use the gold spray before adding the red roses, so that the red and gold stand out against each other.

◄ *All the ingredients for the Christmas basket are readily available; from left to right, fir cones, hydrangea heads, dried roses, gold baubles and poppy seedheads.*

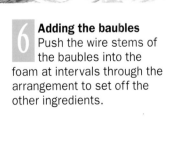

6 Adding the baubles Push the wire stems of the baubles into the foam at intervals through the arrangement to set off the other ingredients.

Flowering House Plants

As an alternative to cut or dried flowers, buy one of these reliable, popular and widely available house plants.

Whether you want instant colour to complement or contrast with your decor, to add a festive touch for a special occasion or just to cheer yourself up, flowering house plants are the perfect choice. They are longer lived than most cut flowers, yet compare favourably in price. For minimal fuss, choose from the easy going, tried-and-true types listed here. Follow care labels, since plant needs vary, but feeding every two weeks when in flower ensures a long-lasting display.

Azalea (*Rhododendron* hybrids)
Size: up to 30 x 30cm (1 x 1ft)
Flowers: white, pink, orange, red, mauve or bicolour, from autumn to spring
Position: cool; bright indirect light
Basic care: keep compost continually moist; mist regularly
Watchpoints: dry air and/or compost can reduce flowering

Cape primrose (*Streptocarpus* hybrids)
Size: up to 30 x 45cm (12 x 18in)
Flowers: trumpet-shaped white, pink, blue, red or purple, from spring to autumn
Position: ordinary room temperature; bright indirect light
Basic care: water freely in spring and summer, moderately in winter; mist occasionally
Watchpoints: protect plants from draughts and from cold air

Cyclamen (*Cyclamen persicum* hybrids)
Size: 10-20cm x 10-20cm (4-8 x 4-8in)
Flowers: white, pink, red or purple, scented in miniature varieties, in autumn and winter
Position: cool; bright indirect light
Basic care: keep the compost continually moist; mist occasionally; dry out corm for summer dormancy, then repot and begin watering in autumn
Watchpoints: water from below to avoid crown rotting; use soft, tepid water

Amaryllis (*Hippeastrum* hybrids)
Size: 30-50cm x 15-20cm (12-20in x 6-8in)
Flowers: huge white, pink, orange or red, trumpet-shaped, in winter or spring
Position: ordinary room temperature; bright indirect light
Basic care: water regularly with tepid water once growth begins and continue until autumn; remove withered leaves and dry off bulb for winter dormancy
Watchpoints: inadequate light in growing period causes non-flowering the following year

Poinsettia (*Euphorbia pulcherrima* hybrids)
Size: up to 45 x 30cm (18 x 12in)
Flowers: white, pink or red flower-like bracts from autumn to spring
Position: ordinary room temperature; maximum light
Basic care: water well; allow compost to dry moderately before re-watering; mist frequently
Watchpoints: warm, dry air can damage flowers; over or under-watering causes leaf fall

Chrysanthemum (*C. morifolium* hybrids)

Size: up to 25 x 20cm (10 x 8in)
Flowers: single or double white, yellow, pink, russet or mauve, all year round
Position: cool; bright indirect light
Basic care: keep compost continually moist; mist occasionally
Watchpoints: all-green buds may fail to open, so be sure to choose plants with buds showing some colour

Zonal geranium (*Pelargonium hortorum* hybrids)

Size: up to 60 x 30cm (2 x 1ft)
Flowers: white, pink, salmon red or mauve ball-shaped, all year round
Position: ordinary room temperature; likes full sun
Basic care: water moderately, sparingly in winter unless plant is in flower
Watchpoints: over-watering rots stems; insufficient light prevents flowers forming

Kalanchöe (*K. blossfeldiana* hybrids)

Size: 15-30 x 10-20cm (6-12 x 4-8in)
Flowers: long-lasting red, yellow or orange clusters, in winter and early spring
Position: ordinary room temperature; direct light
Basic care: water moderately, sparingly for a month after flowering to encourage a rest period
Watchpoints: overwatering plants causes rotting

Christmas cactus (*Zygocactus truncatus*)

Size: up to 30 x 45cm (12 x 18in)
Flowers: rose-pink, in late autumn and winter
Position: ordinary room temperature; bright indirect light, bright light in winter
Basic care: water regularly, but reduce watering after flowering to encourage a rest period; provide high humidity
Watchpoints: changes in light level or temperature can cause buds and/or flowers to drop

African violet (*Saintpaulia* hybrids)

Size: up to 10 x 20cm (4 x 8in)
Flowers: single or double white, pink, red, purple or blue, all year round
Position: ordinary room temperature; bright indirect light, direct light in winter
Basic care: water moderately with tepid water; provide high humidity
Watchpoints: water on the leaves can cause rot, so take care when watering

Tuberous-rooted begonia (*B.* x *tuberhybrida*)

Size: 20-45 x 20-45cm (8-18 x 8-18in)
Flowers: white, pink, yellow, orange or bicoloured, in spring and summer
Position: ordinary room temperature; bright indirect light
Basic care: water moderately in spring and summer, very sparingly in autumn and winter when dormant
Watchpoints: leave dried stems intact when storing over winter – removing them may damage tuber

INDOOR GARDEN BASKET

A wicker basket creatively filled with house plants brings a glimpse of summer into your home during the winter months. Longer lasting than cut flowers, a garden basket gives pleasure for weeks on end.

By making your own garden basket rather than buying a ready-made one, you can personalize the arrangement and select foliage and flower colours to enhance the decor of a particular room. Try to choose plants that share the same light, temperature and water needs, but if you fancy a plant that needs different conditions be prepared to replace it occasionally. Decide where the basket is to be placed before planting it up. If it is to be seen from all sides, put the tallest plant in the centre – for viewing from the front, put the tallest plant at the back.

The flowers and foliage used in this basket like bright but indirect sunlight – rotate the display from time to time so they all have a share of the light. Water your display regularly but lightly to avoid waterlogging, and feed it monthly during the growing season.

A basket of flowering plants is a charming way to add a splash of colour to a room. For a pretty finishing touch, add a ribbon bow in a matching or coordinating colour.

PLANTING UP THE BASKET

YOU WILL NEED

- ❖ BREAD BASKET (38cm/15in diameter)
- ❖ BLACK POLYTHENE
- ❖ GRAVEL
- ❖ Peat-based POTTING COMPOST
- ❖ MAIDENHAIR FERN
- ❖ POLKA DOT PLANT
- ❖ Pink KALANCHOE
- ❖ Pink BUSY LIZZIE (IMPATIENS)
- ❖ VARIEGATED CREEPING FIG AND VARIEGATED IVY
- ❖ SPHAGNUM MOSS

1 Lining the basket Loosely line the basket with thick black polythene, holding it in place with large tacking stitches sewn just under the rim of the basket. Alternatively, place a snug fitting bowl inside.

Ringing the changes
For a seasonal change to this winter basket, you could use primulas in spring, miniature roses or Italian bellflowers in summer, and small chrysanthemums in the autumn.

2 Adding the compost To help prevent waterlogging, place a 1.5cm (½in) layer of gravel in the base. Then cover with a layer of peat-based potting compost.

3 Arranging the plants Keeping the plants in their pots, arrange them in the basket to get the desired effect. Clockwise from the top: pink kalanchoe, polka dot plant, variegated creeping fig, busy Lizzie, variegated ivy and maidenhair fern.

4 Planting up Once you are happy with the arrangement, remove the plants from their pots. Place them one by one in the basket, positioning the tallest plants first. Check that the rootballs come 2.5cm (1in) below the rim to allow for watering.

5 Filling the gaps When all the plants are in position, fill the spaces between the rootballs with more compost, finishing level with the surface of the rootballs. Tap the basket once or twice to firm down.

6 Finishing off To retain moisture, completely cover the potting compost with a layer of sphagnum moss. Water lightly and put the basket on display.

THREE OF A KIND

Think in threes next time you're tempted to buy a pretty little flowering house plant – you'll find a trio of pot plants has more style and makes a greater impact.

It's simple to treble the enjoyment you get from flowering house plants by displaying them in threes rather than individually. Displayed singly, a small flowering plant like a miniature rose is easily overlooked, but give it a couple of companions and the display immediately gains a greater degree of style and impact.

Artists, architects and craftsmen through the ages have taken advantage of the pleasing asymmetry of an arrangement involving odd numbers, particularly three. A display of three flowering plants not only looks more effective but often makes practical sense, too, as you can take full advantage of low-cost seasonal buys. Look for favourites such as miniature daffodils or tulips in the springtime, choose pansies in the winter, or take your pick from any of the wide selection of summer flowers.

Quite a few flowering plants which lend themselves to an indoor display of three – for example, polyanthus, pansies and bulbs – are suitable for planting out in the garden or in a window box once they are past their prime, so you can continue to enjoy them.

More and more plants are being bred in miniature form. These little specimens are just like the rose bushes in a garden, but are a fraction of the size. They look exquisite grouped in three teacups.

FOCUS ON THREE

You can group your trio in one of several ways. The simplest arrangement is to choose three of the same kind of plant with identical coloured blooms – three white cyclamen, perhaps, or some yellow pot chrysanthemums. Or choose the same type of plants but with different coloured flowers – the rich velvety purples and reds of polyanthus, with their bright contrasting eyes, would make a zesty group.

If you like, shift some of the emphasis of your flowery focal point on to the containers by transplanting them into decorative pots – many garden centres are now selling good, inexpensive copies of old terracotta pots.

Alternatively keep the plants in their original pots and put them in one large or three smaller matching containers. Be as inventive as you like with the containers – put three tiny cacti in bloom in matching eggcups, or cluster together three dainty roses in a teapot.

▲ *For a massed effect group three bright-eyed polyanthus in a trug, basket or large bowl. Plants with the same velvety purple blooms are used here, or you could mix different colours.*

PLANT CARE

Stand the plants in a light but not too bright spot, and keep the compost moist. Take care to drain away surplus water when watering plants in an outer container, as most plants hate to sit with wet feet. To encourage a good display, snip off flowers as soon as they start to fade.

▲ *For treble the value, set pretty little polyanthus, still in their original containers, into matching decorative planters.*

◄ *Universal pansies bloom right through winter – transplant them into old-style terracotta pots for a charming and long-lasting old-fashioned threesome. To keep the plants in good shape, remove any faded flowers and straggly growth.*

HYDROCULTURE SPRING BULBS

For flowering bulb displays with a difference, grow the bulbs using hydroculture. Choose a glass planter and you can enjoy watching the roots develop as the flowers bloom.

Bulbs are the perfect plants to add seasonal colour to your home. They are widely available and come in a huge variety of colours and blooms. For a collection of flowering bulbs with a difference, grow them using hydroculture, so you can set them off in attractive glass containers making the most of flower, stem and roots.

Hydroculture is the tried and tested practice of growing bulbs without soil. The bulbs grow just as well as in a soil-nourished environment. In fact, hydroculture has several advantages over conventional growing methods. It is less messy, watering and feeding is simpler and growth is more energetic.

Use a base of stones and gravel, or coloured stones or marbles, for the roots to grow through, and water and soluble plant food to nourish them. Once the bulbs are planted keep them in the dark until the shoots are showing, then you can bring them into the light.

You can buy bulbs that are specially prepared to flower during winter, but for a spring display choose your bulbs in early autumn and select the ones specifically recommended for indoor growing. Hyacinths, crocuses, tulips and daffodils are the most popular choices. These come in all colours of the rainbow, from the lighter whites and golds to exotic deep blues, purples and reds.

If the bulb is adequately supported by a vase all it needs to grow is water. Here, individual hyacinths grow attractively out of special antique hyacinth jars. You can buy reproductions from garden centres and home goods shops.

HYDROPOT BULBS

Hydropot bulbs grow quite happily without soil, but it is a good idea to add something to keep the water slightly acidic so that it stays free from bacteria and algae. Adding a thin layer of charcoal chips is a perfect solution. Layering different sizes and colours of pebbles, gravel or marbles over a thin layer of charcoal at the bottom of the container creates an attractive effect, forming bands of colour that are visible through the sides of the glass.

YOU WILL NEED

- ❖ GLASS CONTAINER
- ❖ CLEAR AND COLOURED MARBLES
- ❖ CHARCOAL CHIPS (optional)
- ❖ BULBS
- ❖ SOLUBLE PLANT FOOD
- ❖ BLACK BIN LINER
- ❖ STRING

1 Preparing the container To keep the water acidic, line the bottom of the container with a thin layer of charcoal chips. Add a thin layer of clear glass marbles and then fill the container with coloured marbles until it is just over half full. Make a shallow depression for each of the bulbs.

2 Planting the bulbs Place a bulb in each depression, so that the necks show well above the marbles. Check that the bulbs don't touch one another. Add a solution of water and soluble plant food until it reaches the base of the bulbs.

3 Storing the bulbs Cut the bin liner so it is the right size to fit over the container and tie it securely at the bottom. Slip it over the container and move it to a cool, dark place – below 10°C (50°F) is ideal. After four weeks, check if the bulbs need more water. Don't allow them to dry out completely.

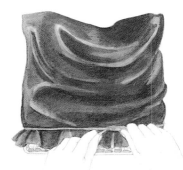

4 Maintaining the bulbs Remove the bag after 8-10 weeks, when the roots are about 1cm (⅜in) long. Place the container where there is some light. Once the buds form you can move them into a spot with direct sunlight. Keep the level of water stable, but be careful not to get any on the necks of the bulbs. Stake any stems that appear fragile.

▲ *Three blue hyacinths, nestling into a bed of coloured marbles, make an attractive display for a mantelpiece or windowsill where the marbles glint in the direct sunlight.*

▶ *Bulbs thrive with remarkably little support. Here, narcissi bloom in a shallow glass vase with only a few well chosen pebbles for the roots to grow around.*

GROWING ORCHIDS

Orchids can be surprisingly successful as greenhouse and even house plants, if you choose the right types and meet their basic needs.

Exotic in origin and appearance, orchids were, until fairly recently, extravagant rarities – as cut flowers confined to special occasions such as weddings and, as plants, to special conservatories and greenhouses. Nowadays, cut orchids such as Singapore orchid and easy-to-grow orchid plants such as cymbidium are sold relatively cheaply in florists and garden centres. If you follow a few guidelines, you can make the most of both types to add an opulent touch to your home.

Most orchids grown as decorative house plants or conservatory plants are epiphytic, found in the wild growing on tree branches or trunks. As well as ordinary feeding roots, most have aerial roots for clinging to their support, and pseudobulbs – bulb-like, thickened stems that store food and water, so they can withstand periods of drought. A few cultivated orchids such as the slipper orchid are ground dwelling, and just have feeding roots.

Most orchid plants are sold in plastic pots, which can be attractively concealed in wicker, moss or ceramic outer pots or baskets. It's fun displaying cut and growing orchids together, and is especially effective if the orchid plants are not in flower.

In a greenhouse you can display orchids with a pendent growth habit, such as cattleyas, in hanging baskets or attached to sections of tree fern, rough cork or tree bark with nylon fishing line.

Pussy willow twigs support delicate but heavy sprays of moth orchid blossom. Most cultivated orchids are epiphytic – in the wild they grow on tree branches or trunks – and require very well drained potting compost.

GROWING ORCHIDS

Light Most tropical orchids need good light but require protection from direct sunlight – except in autumn, when it is essential for future flowering. Generally, the thicker the leaf, the more light an orchid can tolerate; terrestrial slipper orchids require continual light shade. Use net curtains to diffuse light on a sunny windowsill and turn the pots occasionally. In nature, tropical orchids receive at least 10-14 sunlight hours a day. You can supplement low winter light levels or a poorly lit room with artificial lighting; an orchid specialist can advise on the best type of bulb.

Temperature Most orchids flower best at a daytime temperature of 20-21°C (68-70°F), with nighttime temperatures no lower than 16°C (61°F) – cool nights are important. In winter, maintain a minimum temperature of 7-13°C (45-55°F), according to type. Move plants growing on windowsills away from the windows on frosty nights.

Humidity Place pots on a tray of pebbles topped up with water to provide humidity – ideally, 60-70% in summer. Mist spray daily if the temperature rises above 21°C (70°F).

Ventilation Provide good ventilation but avoid cold draughts. You can place orchids outdoors in a sheltered spot and dappled light during summer.

Watering Use tepid, soft water. Keep the potting compost steadily moist but never saturated in the growing season (usually spring and summer) and when in flower. Overwatering is the commonest cause of failure; slipper orchids are particularly vulnerable to overwatering and underwatering. During the rest season (usually winter), reduce watering; this encourages next year's buds to form. Allow the surface to dry out between waterings for oncidiums, miltonias and cattleyas but never allow the potting compost to dry out completely.

Feeding Feed during the growing season and when in bud and flower. Use special orchid fertilizer, ordinary liquid fertilizer or foliar feed, according to instructions. Never feed orchids in the resting season, which varies from type to type, or apply fertilizer to dry potting compost.

Deadheading Cut back the flower stems after the flowers fade. Cut back moth orchid's stems to just below the lowest flower, and new flowers will form on the side shoots that grow from this point.

Repotting This is only necessary if the potting compost rots away or the plant is obviously too big for its pot. Use a special free-draining orchid compost made of a mixture of sphagnum moss, pulverized bark, chopped fern roots, peat, vermiculite and/or perlite. You can use the same or a slightly larger pot; old-fashioned terracotta orchid pots which have drainage holes in the sides and bottom or wire or slatted wood orchid baskets are ideal.

Remove the old potting compost and cut off any dead, brown roots and dead, brown pseudobulbs. Half fill the container with drainage material, then place a layer of moist orchid potting compost on top. Replace the plant, working more potting compost among the roots. Spray the potting compost but do not water for a week; keep warm and humid.

To propagate orchids, divide them when repotting, leaving at least three pseudobulbs or shoots on each division. Pot up and stake.

▶ *Cymbidiums in a range of colours comprise most of this greenhouse display. They are among the easiest orchids to grow and, with their long-lasting blooms, are also the most popular.*

◀ *In terms of display, consider the container as well as the orchid. This twiggy basket, reminiscent of the treetop origins of most epiphytic orchids, is perfect for the job.*

WATCHPOINTS

Hard, dry, brown leaf spots or streaks indicate sun scorch; move to a shadier spot.
Soft brown leaf spots are symptoms of fungal infections; remove the leaf/leaves immediately.
Mildew on leaves means the humidity is too high for the temperature. Raise the temperature or lower the humidity.
Drooping growth indicates inadequate light or incorrect watering.
Non-flowering on a healthy plant is probably due to inadequate light or overfeeding: adjust care or conditions according to type.

Supporting Orchids

Orchid blooms, especially if carried several per spray, can be top heavy. Always make sure you consider the appearance of the support as part of the display.

Supporting top-heavy orchids
To support cattleyas and other top-heavy orchids, wind garden string around upright growth and tie to a thin cane or stake.

Supporting upright stems
Orchids with upright stems and slender flower stalks, such as slipper orchids, should be supported with galvanized wire, U-shaped at the top, then formed into a circle. Place the U just below the neck of flower buds.

◀ *Moth orchids are so called because they resemble graceful moths in flight.*

Supporting arching stems
Insert a cane or stake at an angle and tie a long, arching flower stem to it, using raffia, to support the stem while retaining its natural curves.

73

EASY ORCHIDS TO GROW

The following species and varieties of orchid are reasonably easy to grow, but there are many others available, especially from orchid nurseries. Always check first whether you can meet an orchid's needs – some are definitely prima donnas. Buy a healthy-looking plant in bud and follow the instructions on the care label.

Cattleya The epiphytic corsage orchid has large, often fragrant blooms in a wide range of colours; each flower lasts several weeks. *C. aclandiae* has olive green, red-brown and magenta blooms in autumn and winter; *C. intermedia*, white and purple flowers in summer. Provide consistently high humidity.

Coelogyne These epiphytic orchids carry large numbers of fragrant flowers. *C. cristata* carries white flowers, up to 10cm (4in) across, in winter and early spring. The black orchid (*C. pandurata*), carries large, insect-like, pale-green, black-spotted blooms in summer; it is best grown in a hanging basket.

Cymbidium These are the most popular house plant orchids, with blooms lasting up to six weeks. Easy species include *C. eburneum*, with fragrant, creamy white flowers in early spring, and *C. giganteum*, with yellow-green fragrant flowers in autumn.

Miltonia The epiphytic pansy orchid has velvety, flat-faced blooms lasting up to five weeks in spring and summer. Often sweetly scented, the flowers are richly coloured, with a contrasting blotch. *M. spectabilis* 'Moreliana' has maroon and wine purple blooms; *M. vexillaria*, pale lilac to rosy red, yellow-crested blooms.

Odontoglossum These epiphytic orchids have flowers up to 17.5cm (7in) across, on arching sprays. Flowering season depends on type but can be almost continuous in ideal conditions. The tiger orchid (*O. grande*), one of the easiest orchids to grow, has yellow, brown-banded petals in late summer and autumn; *O. crispum*, white, pink and yellow blooms in winter and spring; and the lily-of-the-valley orchid (*O. puchellum*) fragrant, yellow and white flowers in spring.

Oncidium The epiphytic butterfly orchid has small but spectacular flowers on long, branching stems. *O. crispum* carries chestnut brown and yellow blossoms, up to 40 per stem, in autumn. *O. ornithorynchum* produces stems up to 1m (3ft) long, with up to 50 rosy pink, fragrant blooms in autumn and winter.

Paphiopedilum The terrestrial slipper orchids have a pouch-like lip, and mostly green, white and/or yellow flowers, up to 15cm (6in) across. Each flower lasts up to eight weeks. *P. fairrieanum* has red-striped white petals and a green pouch, in summer and autumn; *P. insigne*, an especially easy species, has multi-coloured flowers in winter.

Phalaenopsis The epiphytic moth orchid has flat-faced flowers on arching stalks, resembling moths in flight. Each flower lasts up to three weeks. *P. stuartiana* has white, pink and reddish purple flowers. There are many hybrids.

◣ *Decorative marks on this moth orchid (Phalaenopsis) serve as guidelines for insects, so aiding pollination.*

◣ *Green orchids make a spectacular addition to any collection. This Cymbidium Fort George 'Lewes' has an especially exotic fascination.*

◥ *Hybrid pansy orchids (Miltonia) produce richly coloured, often sweetly scented flowers during spring and summer that can last up to five weeks.*

Top Ten Foliage Houseplants

Choose one or more of these reliable and robust houseplants to add interest and a welcoming touch to your home.

These tough, evergreen foliage plants can grace coffee tables, shelves or – in the case of larger plants – stand on their own. Put one wherever there's a spot in need of a feature. Feed little and often in the growing season; once every two weeks is enough for most plants. Flowers that appear are insignificant and should be removed, or the plant may become dormant.

1 Boston fern (*Nephrolepis exaltata* 'Bostoniensis')
Size: up to 60 x 60cm (2 x 2ft)
Feature: rosette of handsome fronds
Position: bright but indirect light, warm days and cool nights
Basic care: mist regularly; keep compost continually moist, slightly less so in winter
Watchpoints: dry air and/or compost can cause fronds to die back

2 Spider plant (*Chlorophytum comosum* 'Vittatum')
Size: up to 60cm x 60cm (2 x 2ft), with longer, trailing runners
Feature: rosette of green and white striped leaves, baby plants on leafless runners
Basic care: mist occasionally in warm conditions; water generously in spring and summer, sparingly in autumn and winter
Position: bright but indirect light, ordinary room temperatures
Watchpoints: excessive heat and/or underfeeding can cause leaf tips to turn brown

Clever ideas: train the runners over a wicker, plastic or wire arch

3 Asparagus fern (*Asparagus densiflorus* syn *A. sprengeri*)
Size: up to 90 x 60cm (3 x 2ft)
Feature: arching or trailing fronds
Position: bright but indirect light, warm days and cool nights
Basic care: mist regularly; keep compost continually moist, slightly less so in winter
Watchpoints: excessive heat can cause fronds to turn yellow and die back from the base

4 Weeping fig (*Ficus benjamina* varieties)
Size: up to 3 x 1.2m (10 x 4ft)
Feature: glossy leaves
Position: bright light, average room temperature
Basic care: mist occasionally in warm conditions; water moderately in spring and summer, sparingly in autumn and winter
Watchpoints: insufficient light can cause sudden loss of leaves

1

3

2

4

5 Madagascar dragon tree (*Dracaena marginata*)

Size: up to 1.8 x 1m (6 x 3ft)
Feature: sculptural stems topped by glossy leaf rosettes
Position: light shade, average room temperatures
Basic care: mist regularly; water generously in spring and summer, moderately in autumn and winter
Watchpoints: brown spots on leaves are a sign of underwatering
Clever idea: If the leafy top part becomes ugly and misshapen, you can start again by pruning away the top; the stem will soon form new leafy shoots

6 Dumb cane (*Dieffenbachia picta* or *maculata*)

Size: up to 1m x 60cm (3 x 2ft); leaves to 25cm (10in) long
Feature: long green leaves, intricately patterned with white
Position: moderate light; keep out of direct sunlight
Basic care: mist spray daily throughout the year; water generously in spring and summer, moderately in autumn and winter
Watchpoints: the sap is poisonous and can set up an unpleasant allergic reaction if it comes into contact with the eyes or mouth so keep the plant well out of reach, particularly if there are young children around

7 Sentry palm (*Howea forsteriana*)

Size: up to 3 x 1m (10 x 3ft)
Feature: evergreen fronds
Position: light shade, average room temperatures but keep cool at night, if possible
Basic care: water moderately in spring and summer, sparingly in autumn and winter
Watchpoints: make sure compost does not become waterlogged

8 Fatsia (*Fatsia japonica*)

Size: up to 1.8 x 1.8m (6 x 6ft)
Feature: large, glossy leaves
Position: bright light or semi-shade, average room temperature, cool in winter if possible
Basic care: water regularly in spring and summer, sparingly in autumn and winter
Watchpoints: dry air or exposure to hot summer sun can cause leaves to shrivel

9 Begonia (*Begonia rex*)

Size: up to 45 x 60cm (18 x 24in)
Feature: large, corrugated, angular heart-shaped leaves with richly coloured zones of silver, cream, pink, purple and near black
Position: filtered light
Basic care: moist atmosphere needed, but do not mist; do not allow temperature to drop below 10°C (50°F); water moderately in spring and summer, sparingly in autumn and winter
Watchpoints: water on the leaves causes mildew

10 Prayer plant (*Maranta leuconeura* varieties)

Size: up to 15-20cm (6-8in) high, sprawling over about 30cm (12in)
Feature: oval, shiny, olive-green leaves with red or white veins or brown spots. The leaves stand upright at night
Position: filtered light or shade and a warm, moist atmosphere; keep out of draughts
Basic care: spray frequently throughout the year; do not water compost
Watchpoints: warm dry air and dry roots cause leaves to drop

BOTTLE GARDENS

*For growing and displaying a fascinating collection
of delicate plants with a minimum of maintenance, consider
creating a garden in a bottle.*

The Victorians, who were great plant collectors, discovered that tropical plants needing constant high humidity would thrive in the completely closed environment of a 'Ward Case' – the glass tank that was the precursor of modern-day bottle gardens. In all of these, moisture from plant transpiration condenses on the inside of the glass and runs back into the potting compost, so further watering is rarely needed. The plants are also protected from air pollution, dust and the sudden fluctuations in temperature.

You can buy fully planted bottle gardens but it's cheaper and more fun to create your own. Narrow-necked, clear or green glass bottles such as large carboys are traditional but you can use wine-making demijohns or even old-fashioned sweet jars, as long as the neck is wide enough for small plants to go through. Tinted glass reduces the amount of light reaching the plants – heavily tinted glass is unsuitable. Plastic containers are also unsuitable, as condensation tends to build up on the inside and obscure the plants.

A pale green container adds to the verdant effect of this bottle garden. Place your indoor garden in a light position but not in direct sunlight where delicate foliage will get scorched. Use moss ferns and true ferns – to add colour try variegated or coloured-leaved plants such as polka-dot plant, ribbon plant or one of the variegated arrowhead vines.

small trowel

plant spray

paper funnel

charcoal

muslin

potting compost

pebbles

sand

peat or peat substitute

MATERIALS AND EQUIPMENT

Glass containers should be sturdy, clear, pale green or very light brown to allow light to penetrate. Darkly tinted glass and plastic containers aren't suitable, although small, decorative inserts of stained glass are acceptable.

When choosing plants for a tinted bottle garden, select shade-loving species. To allow for planting and maintenance, make sure the neck or opening of the container is at least 5cm (2in) in diameter. A cork or other stopper in the top, especially of a wide-necked bottle, may help some ferns or waxy-leaved plants to thrive.

You can also use an old-fashioned goldfish bowl; brandy snifter; glass mixing bowl or even fish tank for your bottle garden. Have a glass top cut to fit, but make sure the edges are bevelled.

Drainage material goes on the bottom of the container, so that the potting compost does not become waterlogged. Mix a handful of charcoal chips with clay aggregate pebbles or small washed stone pebbles. The charcoal prevents any standing water from turning sour. Cover the drainage layer with a sheet of muslin or fine gauze to prevent compost washing down into and clogging the drainage.

To avoid smudging the inside of the glass, pour all drainage material and potting compost through a chute or funnel made from a sheet of stiff paper.

Potting compost mix can be made by combining two parts of loam-based potting compost, two parts coarse sand and one part moss peat or peat substitute. This mix ensures the plants remain slow growing yet healthy.

Long-handled tools are easily improvised from simple household utensils – see a selection of tools at the top of the opposite page, but experiment with different ideas while you are developing your bottle gardening skills. A kitchen fork or spoon taped to the end of a small garden cane is useful for planting, and a cotton reel wedged on a cane for firming the potting compost around plants. With a bit of practice, you can manoeuvre young plants into place using two canes, chopstick-fashion, or hold them in a roll of paper, angled through the neck.

Attach a piece of sponge to a cane for wiping away condensation and plant debris. A scalpel or razor blade, similarly attached, can be used for tidying up dead leaves, and a long piece of wire looped at the end is ideal for pulling out dead or overgrown plants and pruned plant material.

A plant spray and a winemaker's plastic funnel and tube are useful for occasional misting or spraying.

▶ *As long as the glass is clear, pale green or very pale brown, you can use almost any type of container you wish for your bottle garden. When the right moisture balance has been reached, insert a cork stopper into broad-necked bottles. Those with very narrow necks can be left open.*

variegated creeping fig

dumb cane

ivy

maidenhair fern

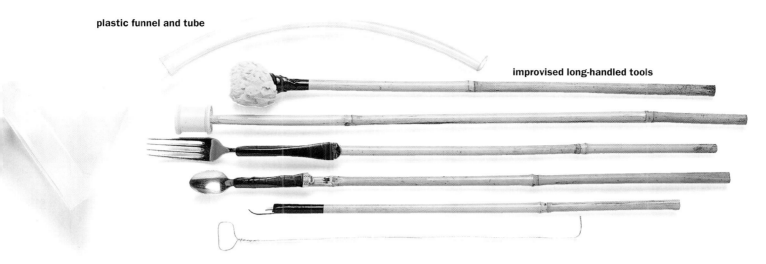

plastic funnel and tube

improvised long-handled tools

BOTTLE GARDEN PLANTS

Select naturally miniature or slow-growing plants which thrive in the same environment – small-leaved foliage plants are ideal. Avoid flowering species as they have a limited season, and the faded flowers quickly rot and are difficult to remove.

Add interest to bottle gardens by choosing a mixture of green, coloured and variegated foliage of different form and texture. As well as creeping ground covers, such as ivy or creeping fig, miniature 'trees' might include tiny palms.

Whether you buy young plants from garden centres or nurseries, take cuttings from friends' house plants or propagate your own seedlings, make sure that the roots are well established before planting.

GREEN/VARIEGATED FOLIAGE

Boston fern (*Nephrolepsis*)
Button fern (*Pellaea rotundifolia*)
Creeping fig (*Ficus pumila*)
Ivy (*Hedera helix* varieties)
Lady fern (*Athyrium felix femina*)
Maidenhair fern (*Asplenium trichomanes*)
Mind-your-own-business (*Soleirolia soleirolii*)
Moss fern (*Selaginella*)
Peperomia (*P. caperata*)

COLOURED FOLIAGE

Aluminium plant (*Pilea cadierei*)
Arrowhead vine (*Syngonium*)
Dumb cane (*Dieffenbachia seguine* varieties)
Golden mind-your-own-business
Polka-dot plant (*Hypoestes phyllostachya*)
Ribbon plant (*Dracaena sanderana*)

peperomia

mind-your-own-business

moss fern

Boston fern

polka-dot plant

PLANTING UP

Before you start, select attractive plants in a range of sizes – taller ones for the back or centre, shorter ones for the front or edges – and plan the arrangement. Thoroughly wash and disinfect the bottle, and let it dry completely, before planting it up. Moulds and other organisms growing on the inside will infect the plants and dirt reduces the light transmission.

For a selection of suitable plants and improvised tools, see advice on previous pages.

1 Preparing for planting Using a paper funnel and small trowel, pour a layer of drainage material on to the base of a clean, dry bottle. Cover the drainage material with a layer of muslin or gauze and add the potting compost mix, spreading it out evenly with a long-handled spoon. For a tiered display, bank up the compost towards the back of the container. Alternatively, make a central mound or a symmetrical mound, to one side of the display.

2 Planting up Make the first planting hole in the potting compost and carefully lower in the plant, holding it between two canes in chopstick-fashion or gripping the root ball between two long-handled spoons.

3 Firming in Insert other plants in the same way until the planting is complete, then firm the compost round the plants with a cotton-reel wedged on to the end of a bamboo cane. Make sure no leaves are covered by the potting compost.

4 Finishing off If you wish, fill bare patches by pressing in small clumps of fresh moss, or with shredded bark or pebbles, using a wire hook, plastic tube or funnel. Lightly mist spray the compost and foliage with tepid water. If the compost is very dry, add a little water through a plastic funnel and tube.

◪ *Modern, transparent terrariums with decorative, stained glass panels are loosely based on popular Victorian designs. Some are fully closed; others, such as this one, have small sections left open, so choose plants accordingly.*

AFTERCARE

Place in a bright place near to a window but not in direct sunlight as solar gain through the glass can kill the plants. You can tell the bottle has reached the right humidity level when there is just a trace of condensation on the glass. If you are growing ferns and waxy-leaved plants, this is the time to insert a stopper.

Check from time to time and remove any excess water with your adapted sponge; only add water if there is no condensation whatsoever.

Be sure to remove damaged or discoloured leaves as soon as they start to appear.

Depending on the growth rate of the plants, your bottle garden should otherwise look after itself for months or even years. Once plants outgrow their space, replanting with young stock is the best solution.

INSTANT IVY SHAPES

Train ivy over a frame to create the ornamental effect of clipped topiary at a fraction of the cost, time and effort of the real thing.

H ere's an easy, economical, indoor gardening project guaranteed to add a touch of class to any room. For best results choose a couple of ivy plants to cover the frame. Select small-leaved, variegated or attractively shaped ivy varieties such as the silver-grey 'Glacier', yellow mottled 'Lutzii' or narrowly lobed, dark green 'Sagittifolia'. Garden centres sell ivies in houseplant and outdoor sections, so check both for the best value. Look for plants with long stems to give your display a good start, and plant the ivy in a nutrient rich potting compost.

Buy metal, plastic, bamboo, rattan or wooden frames from garden centres; specialist suppliers often advertise in gardening magazines. Shapes can be flat or three dimensional and include rings, fans, globes, pyramids, cones, spirals, musical instruments or letters of the alphabet. Ivy is as happy outdoors as inside, so you can put your ivy display on a patio or balcony for the summer months.

Ivy can be trained round wire hoops, with wayward shoots snipped off to keep growth tidy, or it can clamber round a rustic wicker frame.

PLANTING UP A POT

YOU WILL NEED

- ❖ TERRACOTTA FLOWERPOT
- ❖ DRAINAGE MATERIAL such as gravel
- ❖ POTTING COMPOST, loam-based
- ❖ FRAME
- ❖ SOFT GARDEN TWINE
- ❖ TWO IVY PLANTS

☑ *A simple framed cone, available in different sizes from garden centres, is ideal for a trained ivy display. Choose a variegated ivy for a pretty contrast in colour.*

1 Preparing the pot Place a 2.5cm (1in) layer of drainage material in the pot, with a concave piece of broken terracotta over the drainage hole if possible. Cover the drainage layer with compost, deep enough for the top surface of the rootballs to come 2.5-5cm (1-2in) below the pot rim.

▶ *Fun frames for training ivy include those in lyre or heart shapes. To ensure a well defined shape, use a small-leaved variety of ivy for training round all but the simplest of frames.*

2 Planting the ivies Carefully remove the ivies from their pots and place on the potting compost, adjusting the depth as necessary. You can compress the rootballs slightly by rolling them between your hands, but both should fit comfortably in the pot. Add more potting compost, tapping the pot and firming with your hands, to prevent air pockets forming.

3 Adding the frame With the frame central and upright, stick the pointed ends well into the compost. Tease out the ivy stems and tie them, evenly spaced, to the frame. Water lightly and place in an airy, semi-shaded spot for a few days.

TIP

MAKING A RING FRAME

Wrap a wire coathanger around a bucket to form a circle. Twist the ends together into a single foot, splayed out into an S-shaped base, and insert in the pot before filling with nutrient rich compost.

AFTERCARE

Provide good light, especially to retain colour contrast in variegated types. Water and feed regularly during the growing season in spring and summer. Water sparingly in autumn and winter and keep in a cool room. Watch for spider mite and spray with insecticide at the first sign of symptoms: bronzed or yellow blotches, leaf fall and white webbing.

CACTUS DISPLAYS

Compact, undemanding and slow growing, small cacti make ideal collector's plants, while a large specimen cactus can add immense character to a room.

With their boldly sculptural, abstract forms, desert cacti are perfect for enhancing modern or Mediterranean-style decors and can add an unexpected pleasant touch to more traditional ones. Small plants are widely and cheaply available; large specimens, because of their age, tend to be costly. Succulents – similar to cacti but lacking their tiny, spiny or hairy cushion-like aereoles – are often included in a collection for their contrasting texture and form.

The level of light is all important if these fascinating plants are to thrive. Most desert cacti and succulents need year-round maximum sunlight with, ideally, a spell outdoors in summer and cool winters. Sunny windowsills are best but, if light levels are low, instead collect forest cacti – Christmas cacti, Easter cacti or epiphyllums, with their huge, often fragrant blooms – which do well in lower light levels.

Most desert cacti and succulents need dry air, regular watering and feeding in spring and summer and just enough water the rest of the year to prevent the potting compost drying out. Forest cacti prefer a steadier supply of water and food, and shade and humidity in summer. Use specially formulated cactus fertilizer and repot, if necessary, with free-draining cactus potting compost, protecting your hands with stout gloves and thickly folded newspaper wrapped round the plant.

The myth that cacti flower only once in seven years is just that – a myth. Many cacti produce brilliantly coloured flowers when still young.

Unique among house plants, cacti and succulents have an abstract, sculptural quality – symmetrical or asymmetrical, tall and elegant or even humorously dumpy. In this clever trompe l'oeil, living cacti are combined with a painted cacti backdrop.

GETTING STARTED

To start off your cactus collection you can concentrate on one group of closely related cacti or go for a more varied approach, combining specimens of several varieties. Larger garden centres usually offer a reasonable selection. If you're keen, there are specialist cacti nurseries, clubs and societies where you can find out about and purchase rarer varieties of cactus.

Cacti are ideal for encouraging children's interest in plants. Start them off with miniature cacti and succulents – two-toned grafted cacti such as gymnocalycium, with their brightly coloured tops, are specially fascinating – either in individual pots or as a desert dish garden. Make sure gloves are worn when caring for spiny cacti as the spines can inflict a nasty injury.

◀ *Pep up and personalize your collection with colour-coordinated designer containers. These cacti and succulents are grown in plastic pots but displayed in handpainted terracotta outer pots decorated with '50s motifs. You can also chalk or colourwash terracotta to match the room, or buy glazed ceramic pots or outer pots.*

▼ *A 'little and large' pair of prickly pears (opuntias) enhance their quarry tile and sunny whitewashed setting. Mature opuntias grown in their natural environment produce edible fruit; indoors, specimen-sized opuntias need heavy pots to counterbalance their height and weight.*

◪ *Desert cacti and sunny yellow decor make a natural duo. Display rows of cacti on windowsills or shelves – glass shelves in a sunny window would be perfect – and clusters of cacti on tables. Turn cacti from time to time to ensure an even exposure to light; if they are in a moderately lit spot, return them regularly to a sunny windowsill for rest and recovery.*

DECORATING TERRACOTTA POTS

*Decorate plain clay pots with motifs made
from modelling clay, then add a flourish with a colour
wash to suit your decorating style.*

U nglazed terracotta pots are perfect candidates for a touch of decorative detailing. Although the colour and texture of baked clay is attractive in itself, by adding small modelling clay details, such as flowers or hearts, and a wash of diluted paint you can enhance these qualities and still retain the charm of the original material. Because the clay's surface is porous, the paint sinks into it so that its characteristic rough texture remains visible.

Self-hardening terracotta modelling clay, available from art shops, is ideal for making the decorative motifs. As well as looking like the real thing, it is easy to handle and dries quickly. All you need to do is glue the motifs in place, then brush over the pot with the colour wash – the added motifs look like part of the original fired pottery. Water-based paints are ideal for indoor pots, but for pots destined for outdoor use, thinned oil-based paint is more durable.

*Straightforward
motifs, like these
flowers, crowns
and heart, work
best, as they
complement the
simple charm of
the pots.*

MAKING CLAY POT MOTIFS

YOU WILL NEED

- ❖ UNGLAZED TERRACOTTA POT
- ❖ TERRACOTTA MODELLING CLAY
- ❖ SPRAY MISTER (optional)
- ❖ WORK BOARD
- ❖ SMALL CRAFT KNIFE
- ❖ FOOD CUTTERS
- ❖ EPOXY RESIN ADHESIVE
- ❖ LOW-TACK MASKING TAPE
- ❖ WATER-BASED PAINTS
- ❖ SMALL PAINT BRUSH
- ❖ PENCIL
- ❖ OLD NEWSPAPERS

Take the simple clay motifs shown here as inspiration, or create your own designs. Food cutters are useful for shaping the clay motifs and are a good source of design ideas. The instructions here show you how to decorate a pot with a simple flower motif, but the basic technique is the same for any design.

2 **Making a flower motif** Dampen the palm of your hand and flatten a ball of modelling clay into a disc 5cm (2in) in diameter and 6mm (¼in) thick. Either use a food cutter to cut out a shape from the clay, or to make a flower motif mark the petals with a knife by cutting five equally spaced triangular notches around the edge and moulding the clay into petal shapes. Roll a small piece of clay into a ball and press it firmly but gently on to the flower centre.

1 **Preparing the materials** Scrub the pots to remove dirt and allow them to dry. Knead a small amount of clay on a work board until it is pliable. If the clay starts to dry out while you work, use a spray mister to dampen it with water.

3 **Positioning the motif** With a craft knife point, scratch the back of the motif to create a key for the adhesive. Lay the motif in position on the pot and gently press it to fit round the curve of the pot. Draw round the motif with a pencil to mark its position. Carefully remove the motif and leave it to dry for up to 24 hours.

4 **Applying the motif** Mix the epoxy resin and spread a little on the back of the motif and within the pencil outline on the pot. (If part of the motif is to stand up above the pot rim, apply the adhesive to the contact area only.) When the adhesive becomes tacky, hold the motif in place with tape until dry. Remove any excess adhesive.

5 **Painting the pot** In a paint kettle or dish, dilute the paint with equal amounts of water and brush it over the clay surface, taking the colour over to the inside of the pot to below soil level. Leave the pot to dry, then re-apply another coat of colour if necessary.

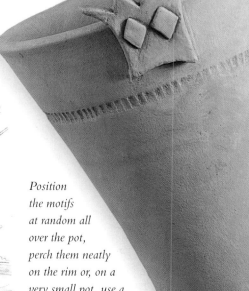

Position the motifs at random all over the pot, perch them neatly on the rim or, on a very small pot, use a single dainty motif.

GROUPING HOUSE PLANTS

Displaying house plants in groups, whether informal clusters or formal geometric patterns, creates eye-catching impact, and the house plants themselves can benefit from the pleasures of communal life together.

I n nature, wild plants intermingle beautifully of their own accord, using each other for shelter, shade, support and humidity. In the home, it's an easy job to re-create the charm of a natural looking plant group. Alternatively, you can follow a more formal approach, with pairs, trios or rows of house plants spaced equally apart, like chessmen on a chessboard. You can combine widely different kinds of house plants, display a collection of one broad type such as ferns, cacti or bromeliads, or narrow the range to just one genus – African violets, for example, or geraniums.

Combining foliage and flowering house plants is always a good idea, since flowering house plants often have dull leaves and foliage plants benefit from adjacent floral colour. Then, too, the foliage house plants can act as a permanent backdrop for a series of short-lived, cheap and cheerful flowering house plants, such as chrysanthemums or miniature roses, that come and go.

When grouping plants, try to site them where their needs for light and heat are met, as well as considering their decorative potential. On a practical level, it's easier to care for house plants grouped according to needs. Mist-spraying thin-leaved foliage plants such as ferns, for example, or feeding cacti and succulents with special fertilizer is easier if they're all collected in one place.

Standing smartly to attention in their wirework holder, these three dwarf hebes reflect the formality of the dining room decor. The terracotta flowerpots add a sense of permanence to the show, and their matching saucers protect the table from water marks.

◄ Some like it hot
and a warm, humid bathroom makes a perfect home for this community of ferns. Included are dramatic stag's-horn ferns, shuttlecock-shaped bird's-nest ferns, delicate maidenhair ferns and Boston ferns, with trailing ivy adding a vertical accent over the bath.

▼ Filling a sunny window
with ivy and Persian violets in twiggy planters, interspersed with brilliant blue glassware, creates an interesting and spectacular effect. Transparent glass shelves allow maximum light to reach the plants and the room, and form a delicately airy, floating base for the display.

▲ Joining the jovial mixture of house plants, the decorative brass watering can and mist sprayer form part of this display. Those in the trough enjoy high humidity while the succulent donkey's tail, cascading over the table, prefers a drier lifestyle.

◄ A prickly collection of miniature cacti and succulents makes a movable feast in a decorative wirework basket. They can easily be transported round the room, or from room to room, to act as a table centrepiece or a windowsill decoration.

Basic House Plant Care

Correct watering and feeding makes for handsome, healthy and long-lived house plants.

The difference between a house plant that glows with good health and one that struggles to survive and perhaps even dies is often simply a matter of how you feed and water it. Watering and feeding routines are seasonal, and an increase or decrease in one often means a matching adjustment in the other.

The golden rule is: if in doubt, use restraint. More house plants are killed by overwatering than anything else and too much food is more harmful than too little. The information here is for general guidance – always read the care label, and keep it for future reference when you buy a new plant, as a few plants have very specific needs.

Watering

How often you water varies according to plant, compost, pot, season and surroundings.

Plant There are a few plants, for example azaleas, that need continually wet potting compost. Generally, thin- or large-leaved plants and quick-growing plants need frequent watering. Cacti, succulents and plants with thick, fleshy or waxy leaves, grey-leaved plants and slow-growing plants need less.

Compost Plants in peat-based compost need more frequent watering than those in loam-based compost.

Container Plants in small pots or pots made from unglazed clay need more frequent watering than those in large plastic pots. A pot filled with roots needs generous watering.

Season Growing and flowering plants need watering weekly, twice weekly or even daily. Dormant plants can go for a week, a fortnight or, with cacti, up to a month without water. Most plants grow in spring and summer but some (such as cyclamen) grow in winter.

Surroundings Plants in hot (especially centrally heated) dry conditions need more frequent watering than those in cool humid ones.

WATERING TIPS

Fill your watering can and leave it to stand so the water you use is at room temperature.

❖

In cool rooms, water in the morning to prevent fungal infections.

❖

If your pot doesn't have drainage holes, water carefully and pour off any excess at once.

❖

After watering, empty saucers and drip trays after 30 minutes; most plants don't like sitting in water.

❖

In areas with hard water, collect rainwater, or boil and cool tap water, for use with lime-haters such as azaleas.

❖

When should you water?

Moisture meters and moisture-sensitive tabs can measure the exact water content of potting compost, but you can usually tell all you need to know by a quick look, or by feeling the compost.

Plants in flower Keep the compost continually moist, but not soaking; water when it starts to look pale, powdery and dry.

Cacti and succulents When growing, let the top 1cm (⅜in) of compost dry out between watering; when dormant, let it dry out almost completely – water only if the plant starts to shrivel.

Foliage plants (especially vigorous climbers and plants with extensive roots and large leaves) In the growing season, water often enough to keep the potting compost continually moist. When dormant, let the top 1cm (⅜in) dry out between watering.

Where to water

For many plants, where you apply the water is as important as when you water. If in doubt, water from below. Plants that like a humid atmosphere benefit from an occasional mist-spray.

Watering from below African violets, cyclamen and sinningias (gloxinias) may rot if watered from above. Instead, stand the plant in a deep saucer of water, or immerse the pots in water up to just below the potting compost surface. Leave until the surface looks wet then drain thoroughly.

Watering from above Insert the tip of the spout under any leaves; pour until water reaches the pot rim (less when the plant is dormant).

Watering bromeliads With certain plants such as bromeliads, water directly into the central, vase-shaped leaf rosette.

Holiday watering care

Before you go on holiday, group plants out of direct sunlight to benefit from increased humidity and to reduce water loss through the leaves. When repotting, prepare for periods of infrequent watering by mixing water-retentive gels into the compost.

If your plants are in plastic pots, place them on capillary matting on a draining board. Fill a bowl or the sink with water, and immerse one end of the matting in water.

For plants that need a good supply of water at the roots, use plastic self-watering containers and leave them well topped up with water.

Group plants round a water-filled bowl. Run wicks of old nylon tights or capillary matting strips from the water up into the drainage holes, pulling them through with tweezers.

Place well watered, small plants in clear polythene bags – make sure the bags don't rest on the plant by inserting two or three canes in the compost first, and blowing into the bags to inflate them before fastening them tightly.

Put damp capillary matting in a bath. Place plants on top and leave the tap dripping gently.

Push a special clay cone, attached to a plastic tube or wick, into the potting compost, and place the other end of the tube in water.

Feeding

Feed growing and flowering plants regularly. Dormant plants, seedlings and newly rooted cuttings need little or no food. Newly bought or repotted plants have enough food for about eight weeks.

Types of fertilizer

General, all-purpose or balanced feeds are fine for most plants. You can use potash-rich fertilizers, such as tomato fertilizer, to boost flowering, and nitrogen-rich fertilizers for leafy growth. There are special fertilizers for African violets, cacti, orchids, citrus trees, bonsai and lime-haters; and seasonal fertilizers for, say, a quick spring boost.

Methods of application

❖ Concentrated liquid and soluble powder fertilizers, diluted in water according to instructions, are easy to use and can be varied according to the plant's need. Add the fertilizer to the watering can when watering.
❖ Insoluble, slow-release granules provide nutrients for up to four months. Add to compost when repotting.
❖ Insoluble, quick-acting powder, granules and crystals are sprinkled on the potting compost surface. They are less available to plant roots than soluble fertilizers.
❖ Slow-release tablets and spikes pushed in the compost are easy to use, but encourage uneven root growth and the amount of fertilizer released cannot be varied.
❖ Liquid foliar feeds, applied with a spray gun or impregnated sponge, give plants an instant boost, but are not suitable for long term use.

FEEDING TIPS

Use fertilizer according to instructions. Don't feed too often, or give too strong a solution – rather than doing good, you are likely to damage the plant's roots.

❖

Always water before you feed – never add fertilizer to a dry compost. Never feed plants when they are dormant.

❖

Apply fertilizer to healthy plants: if a plant is ailing, do not assume it is malnourished. It's far more likely to be incorrect watering, or a pest or disease – treat the problem before feeding.

❖

Pruning House Plants

Correct pruning and training result in compact growth and healthy plants.

Many house plants benefit from regular pruning to keep them compact, well balanced and within the allotted space. Pruning also aids rejuvenation, encouraging the production of young, healthy growth, which in turn often carries the best flowers and foliage.

House plants which in their natural environment would twine round, cling to or scramble through nearby shrubs, need training to supports to keep them tidy and encourage flowering. And a few non-climbers with heavy flowers and slender stems also benefit from support.

Types of pruning

Pruning ranges from tipping (removing just the tiny tips of new shoots) and light pruning (removing up to half of the previous season's new growth) to hard pruning (removing up to three-quarters of the plant's growth). When pruning always use a sharp knife or secateurs to avoid crushing the plant's stems.

Tipping

Also called stopping or pinching out, tipping encourages dormant buds lower down the stem to break into growth. This results in branching, compact growth and more (although delayed) blooms on flowering plants. Plants such as chrysanthemums, coleus, cane begonias, pelargoniums and busy Lizzies, which are liable to grow tall and spindly, benefit from tipping. The main time to tip is mid spring to early summer, but quick-growing plants may need tipping several times during the growing season. With newly rooted cuttings, the first tipping of the main stem is followed by tipping the side shoots that develop, then the sub-side shoots.

How to tip Only tip actively growing plants. Use your thumb and fingers, or a pair of scissors, to remove the 6-12mm (¼-½in) long growing tips of new shoots and, if the growth points are close together, one or two buds, leaves or pairs of leaves below the growing tip.

Light pruning

This involves removing some of the new growth but leaving the older growth intact. Small, young but potentially large plants such as bougainvilleas can be light pruned until they fill their allotted space, then hard pruned. If in doubt, light pruning house plants is safer than hard pruning.

Light prune plants in late winter or early spring, just before repotting, or in autumn before their winter dormancy. Generally, the weaker the growth, the harder you prune.

How to light prune Cut back the tips of the previous year's growth by up to half its length. The new growth can be distinguished because it is usually softer and/or a different colour from the older growth.

Pruning plants

Always make a tidy, slanting cut, about 6mm (¼in) above an outward facing bud, leaf or shoot; angle the cut downwards, away from the bud (**a**); (**b**) too close to bud; (**c**) too far from bud; (**d**) angled in wrong direction.

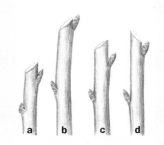

Hard pruning

Plants which flower only on new growth, such as passion flower, poinsettias and jasmine, need annual hard pruning to ensure a good show of flowers. Hard pruning involves removing half to three-quarters of the new growth. With rampant-growing house plants, regular pruning also prevents dense, tangled growth and allows light and air to reach and ripen the young growth.

Prune in late winter or early spring, just before repotting, or in autumn, before plants begin their winter dormancy.

How to hard prune Prune both the main stems and side growth of rampant climbers; you can cut side growths flush with the main stems or leave a 2.5cm (1in) spur with one or two buds or leaves attached. Some shrubby house plants, such as oleander, with leafless stems, can be cut back well into old wood, to encourage them to sprout from the base.

MAINTENANCE PRUNING

Always remove the following stems or shoots back to a growth point or healthy stem:

❖

Weak, dead, leafless and diseased stems.

❖

Crossing shoots, leaving the better placed of the two; excessively long shoots that give an unbalanced look.

❖

All-green shoots on variegated plants.

❖

Stems with pale, small and/or weak leaves.

❖

Overcrowded stems in the centre of the plant.

Training

Training involves providing firm supports and tying in stems as they grow, to display flowers and foliage to best advantage. Even house plants that cling by aerial roots still need initial tying in until they become established. Always match the strength and size of support to the expected size and weight of the plant.

Trellis

Wood, cane, plastic-coated wire and plastic trellis, in rectangular or fan-shaped panels, is available from garden centres, or you can make your own. Small panels have feet for inserting into the pot; large panels are fixed to battens nailed to walls. Trellis suits climbers such as stephanotis and jasmine.

Types of supports

Wire

Hoops or rings made of sturdy wire and inserted into the pot suit climbers with flexible stems such as passion flower, plumbago, bougainvillea and hoya. Fixed to a brick wall with vine eyes, or suspended from cup hooks or screw eyes, wire can be shaped to support a large plant.

Topiary frames

Sturdy wire globes, obelisks and other more unusually shaped frames – useful for training small-leaved varieties of ivy or creeping fig for instant topiary – are available from specialist garden suppliers.

Canes

Bamboo poles can be inserted at equal spacings around the edge of a pot, with one or more horizontal rows of twine stretched round them, to form a supporting cage. Tripods made of three or four bamboo poles inserted into the pot and tied tightly at the top can support climbers such as grape ivy or kangaroo vine. Similar to canes but smaller are green pea sticks.

Moss poles

These can be bought from garden centres or homemade – see below for details on how to do this. Train aerial-rooting climbers such as philodendron, ivy, devil's ivy, creeping fig and Swiss cheese plant up moss poles. Keep the moss continually moist and the aerial roots will work their way into it.

Making a moss pole

1 Shaping the wire
Roll a rectangular piece of chicken wire into a tubular shape and bend the loose ends into the centre of the tube. Seal one end of the tube by bending over the chicken wire.

2 Filling the tube
Cut open the wire at the other end of the tube and bend it back. Fill the empty tube with sphagnum moss using a broom handle to push it in. Make sure it is packed in tightly. Close the end of the tube by bending the wire back. Stand the tube in the centre of a plant pot and wedge it in place with potting mixture.

3 Attaching a climbing plant
Pot a climbing plant in the mixture and attach its stems to the moss pole with wire pegs. Mist-spray regularly.

> ## YOU WILL NEED
> ❖ CHICKEN WIRE
> ❖ WIRE CUTTERS
> ❖ SPHAGNUM MOSS
> ❖ BROOM HANDLE
> ❖ POTTING MIXTURE
> ❖ PLANT POT
> ❖ CLIMBING HOUSE PLANT
> ❖ WIRE PEGS

Types of ties

Garden twine and **raffia spools** are low cost and ideal for soft stems. Cut them into short lengths or use longer lengths to connect canes encircling a plant.
Paper-coated wire plant ties, or twists, come in pre-cut lengths and reels, and are useful for tying in tough, woody stems.
Metal plant rings are ideal for attaching plants with thin stems to canes or wires.
Green plastic ties are notched for easy fixing, and can be adjusted as the plant grows and the stem diameter increases. Use them with tough, woody stems.

TIP
TRAINING TIPS
Provide supports before plants get out of control.

❖

Always handle plant stems gently, and tie stems loosely to supports.

❖

Check ties regularly and adjust as necessary, especially with quick-growing plants.

❖

Use a support framework, rather than a single cane, if possible.

House Plant Troubleshooter

A few simple precautions and remedies ensure your house plants remain in the best condition.

In addition to benefiting from correct feeding and watering, house plants have specific needs for heat, light and humidity. If kept in ideal conditions, they provide a long-lasting display of healthy flowers and foliage. Plant needs vary, and basic care information is usually given on labels inserted into the pot. The following general guide to common plant problems is useful if your plants begin to look unhealthy.

The right temperature

❖ Temperature needs are seasonal and reflect a plant's natural growth cycle – usually active growth during the spring and summer months and dormancy in the autumn and winter months. Provide warmth for most actively growing and flowering house plants, and cooler temperatures for dormant ones. House plants, such as Italian bellflower, that lose their leaves when dormant need quite cool temperatures.

❖ Provide cool but frost-free temperatures for winter-flowering hardy or nearly hardy house plants such as azaleas, polyanthus, forced hyacinths and daffodils, to prevent premature withering of the blooms.

❖ House plants are more liable to suffer from too much heat than too little – particularly in houses with central heating during the winter. If in doubt, lower the temperature or move the plant to a cooler spot.

❖ Keep house plants well away from direct sources of heat such as radiators.

❖ Try to avoid wildly fluctuating temperatures, though a drop in night temperatures is often beneficial, especially in winter. Don't move house plants between rooms of very different temperatures.

❖ House plants left on windowsills at night in cold weather can occasionally suffer from frost damage, especially if the plant is behind closed curtains that prevent any heat from reaching it.

❖ Provide draught-free ventilation, particularly in hot weather.

The right light

❖ Display cacti, succulents such as Aloe varieties and most plants with furry, grey or waxy leaves in plenty of direct sunlight all year round.

❖ House plants need more light when in bud or flowering than when resting, so move them closer to a window, if necessary.

❖ The thinner the leaf, the more you must protect the plant from direct sunlight. The delicate leafy fronds of maidenhair fern, for example, shrivel up when exposed to direct sunlight for long periods.

❖ Provide plenty of light for coloured leaved and variegated house plants. Prolonged exposure to direct sunlight scorches or bleaches the white or yellow leaf area in some varieties.

❖ To prevent lopsided growth towards the light give house plants growing near a directional source of light such as a window a quarter turn every few days.

❖ In winter, when light levels are low, move light tolerant house plants closer to a window.

❖ In summer, only cacti and some succulents can stand the intense light on a windowsill that gets full sunlight. Move other house plants back or shield from sun with netting or blinds.

❖ House plants benefit from being put outdoors in summer, in a sunny or shaded spot as appropriate.

❖ Shrubby flowering plants such as oleander benefit from sunlight ripening the wood, which encourages flowering during the next season.

Humidity hints

❖ The thinner the leaf, the more humid the conditions the plant likes, especially in high temperatures.

❖ Group humidity loving house plants together to create a beneficial humid micro-climate.

❖ Place a humidity loving plant on a pebble-filled tray or shallow dish kept topped up with water.

❖ Use mist sprayers often to spray leaves of humidity loving house plants.

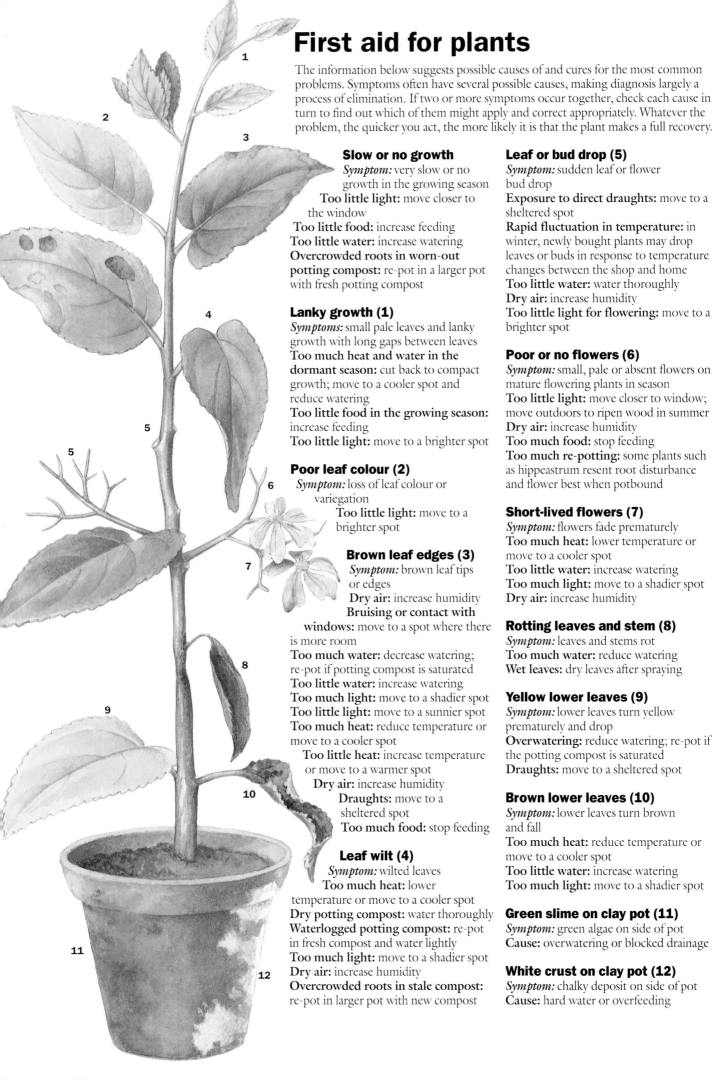

First aid for plants

The information below suggests possible causes of and cures for the most common problems. Symptoms often have several possible causes, making diagnosis largely a process of elimination. If two or more symptoms occur together, check each cause in turn to find out which of them might apply and correct appropriately. Whatever the problem, the quicker you act, the more likely it is that the plant makes a full recovery.

Slow or no growth

Symptom: very slow or no growth in the growing season
Too little light: move closer to the window
Too little food: increase feeding
Too little water: increase watering
Overcrowded roots in worn-out potting compost: re-pot in a larger pot with fresh potting compost

Lanky growth (1)

Symptoms: small pale leaves and lanky growth with long gaps between leaves
Too much heat and water in the dormant season: cut back to compact growth; move to a cooler spot and reduce watering
Too little food in the growing season: increase feeding
Too little light: move to a brighter spot

Poor leaf colour (2)

Symptom: loss of leaf colour or variegation
Too little light: move to a brighter spot

Brown leaf edges (3)

Symptom: brown leaf tips or edges
Dry air: increase humidity
Bruising or contact with windows: move to a spot where there is more room
Too much water: decrease watering; re-pot if potting compost is saturated
Too little water: increase watering
Too much light: move to a shadier spot
Too little light: move to a sunnier spot
Too much heat: reduce temperature or move to a cooler spot
Too little heat: increase temperature or move to a warmer spot
Dry air: increase humidity
Draughts: move to a sheltered spot
Too much food: stop feeding

Leaf wilt (4)

Symptom: wilted leaves
Too much heat: lower temperature or move to a cooler spot
Dry potting compost: water thoroughly
Waterlogged potting compost: re-pot in fresh compost and water lightly
Too much light: move to a shadier spot
Dry air: increase humidity
Overcrowded roots in stale compost: re-pot in larger pot with new compost

Leaf or bud drop (5)

Symptom: sudden leaf or flower bud drop
Exposure to direct draughts: move to a sheltered spot
Rapid fluctuation in temperature: in winter, newly bought plants may drop leaves or buds in response to temperature changes between the shop and home
Too little water: water thoroughly
Dry air: increase humidity
Too little light for flowering: move to a brighter spot

Poor or no flowers (6)

Symptom: small, pale or absent flowers on mature flowering plants in season
Too little light: move closer to window; move outdoors to ripen wood in summer
Dry air: increase humidity
Too much food: stop feeding
Too much re-potting: some plants such as hippeastrum resent root disturbance and flower best when potbound

Short-lived flowers (7)

Symptom: flowers fade prematurely
Too much heat: lower temperature or move to a cooler spot
Too little water: increase watering
Too much light: move to a shadier spot
Dry air: increase humidity

Rotting leaves and stem (8)

Symptom: leaves and stems rot
Too much water: reduce watering
Wet leaves: dry leaves after spraying

Yellow lower leaves (9)

Symptom: lower leaves turn yellow prematurely and drop
Overwatering: reduce watering; re-pot if the potting compost is saturated
Draughts: move to a sheltered spot

Brown lower leaves (10)

Symptom: lower leaves turn brown and fall
Too much heat: reduce temperature or move to a cooler spot
Too little water: increase watering
Too much light: move to a shadier spot

Green slime on clay pot (11)

Symptom: green algae on side of pot
Cause: overwatering or blocked drainage

White crust on clay pot (12)

Symptom: chalky deposit on side of pot
Cause: hard water or overfeeding

House Plant Pests

Quick action can often save infested house plants and prevent the problem spreading.

Prevention is the best cure – making sure your house plants get the right amount of food, water, heat and light ensures tough, sturdy growth, and a strong healthy plant is more resistant to pest attacks. But even with the best care, problems can occur. If they do, correct identification, quick response and using the right fungicide or pesticide are vital in restoring diseased or infested house plants to their prime. This approach also stops the problem spreading to other house plants and becoming out-of-control.

The ten most common pests

Aphids (greenfly)
Green, black, grey or orange, tiny, sap-sucking insects, some with wings, attack soft, young leaves, tips and flowerbuds and spread incurable viruses.
Symptoms: stunted, distorted growth; sticky honeydew covered in sooty mould.
Treatment: rub off small colonies; remove and destroy heavily infested tips; spray regularly with insecticide.

Cyclamen mites
Too small to be seen individually, heavy infestations of these sap-sucking insects and their pale eggs look like dust on leaf undersides, especially on cyclamen, African violets, busy Lizzies, ivies and geraniums.
Symptoms: twisted, brittle stems and leaves, curled leaf edges, stunted growth, shrivelled flowerbuds and loss of flower colour.
Treatment: remove and destroy infested parts; spray regularly with insecticide; destroy heavily infested plants.

Earwigs
These shiny, dark-brown, narrow insects with pincer-like tails appear mainly at night.
Symptoms: ragged holes and edges on leaves and petals.
Treatment: check leaf undersides or shake plant, picking off and destroying earwigs.

Leaf miners
Thin, sap-sucking grubs burrow through leaves, leaving pale markings and weakening the plant.
Treatment: remove and destroy infested leaves; spray regularly with insecticide.

Mealy bugs
Oval, pale pink pests form large, fluffy white colonies on leaf axils, stems and leaf undersides.
Symptoms: rapid wilting, yellowing, prematurely falling leaves, covered in honeydew and sooty mould.
Treatment: wipe light infestations off with damp cloth, stiff paint brush or cotton bud soaked with methylated spirits. Spray heavy infestations regularly with insecticide.

Red spider mites
Minute, red, sap-sucking insects spin silky webs on leaf undersides.
Symptoms: yellow, mottled, curled, black-dotted leaves; premature leaf fall; stunted new growth; black flowerbuds.
Treatment: provide a cooler, more humid atmosphere; remove and destroy infested growth; spray with insecticide.

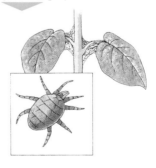

Scale insects
Small, brown, waxy shields cover sap-sucking insects on leaf undersides, especially along veins and midribs.
Symptoms: yellow, sticky, puckered leaves covered in honeydew and sooty mould.
Treatment: wipe off with a damp cloth or cotton wool soaked in methylated spirits, then spray with insecticide.

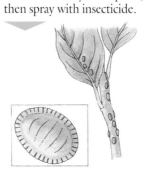

Thrips
These tiny black, jumping, sap-sucking insects attack begonias, fuchsias and crotons.
Symptoms: mottled or silvery streaks on leaves; white-spotted, distorted flowers; black-speckled leaves and blooms; stunted growth.
Treatment: remove and destroy badly infected flowers and leaves; spray regularly with insecticide.

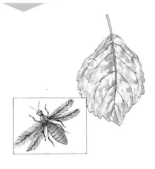

Vine weevils
The large white grubs of these leaf-chewing beetles attack roots, bulbs and tubers.
Symptoms: plants wilt and die for no obvious reason.
Treatment: hand-pick and destroy beetles; spray potting compost with insecticide; discard and destroy badly infested plants.

Whitefly
Rapidly spreading, white, moth-like insects, especially on busy Lizzies, begonias, fuchsias and geraniums; immature, green larvae found on leaf undersides.
Symptoms: yellow leaves covered in honeydew, premature leaf fall, weak growth.
Treatment: spray repeatedly with insecticide.

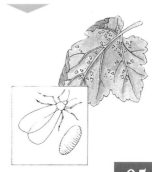

House plant diseases

Always check new house plants for signs of disease (or pests) before you take them into your house. Early identification of a diseased plant is vital. When you have removed affected leaves or flowers from a plant, burn them if possible to avoid spreading the disease.

The ten most common diseases

Blackleg
Symptoms: stems of infected plants, especially pelargoniums, turn black and rot at the base.
Treatment: reduce watering and ensure free-draining potting compost; use hormone rooting powder containing fungicide; discard infected plants, though you can take cuttings from sound parts above the infected stem.

Botrytis (grey mould)
Symptoms: grey, fluffy mould covers leaves, stems, flowerbuds and flowers, especially of soft-leaved plants.
Treatment: increase air circulation and decrease humidity and watering; try to avoid wetting leaves when watering; remove and destroy infected parts and spray or dust with fungicide; discard badly infected plants.

Crown and stem rot
Symptoms: soft, rotting stems or central leaves of crown-forming plants such as many bromeliads.
Treatment: cut away rotten parts of lightly infected plants; spray or dust with fungicide, increase heat and ventilation; reduce watering; remove and destroy badly infected plants.

Leafspot
Symptoms: brown, often yellow-edged, damp spots enlarge and spread, killing leaves.
Treatment: remove and destroy infected leaves, spray or dust with fungicide and reduce humidity and watering; try to avoid wetting leaves when watering.

Oedema (corky scab)
Symptoms: hard, corky growths on leaf undersides.
Treatment: remove affected leaves; re-pot in free-draining potting compost and decrease watering.

Powdery mildew
Symptoms: white, powdery, non-fluffy coating on leaf surfaces, spreading to flowers.
Treatment: remove and destroy badly infected parts; spray or dust with fungicide; improve ventilation.

Root rot
Symptoms: leaves wilt and turn yellow then brown and finally collapse completely; roots are slimy and smell offensive; African violets, succulents, palms and begonias are particularly vulnerable.
Prevention/cure: leave lightly infected plants out of their pots for 1-2 days, trim off brown, slimy roots and damaged stems or leaves; dust cut surfaces with fungicide; re-pot in drier, free-draining potting compost and spray with fungicide; destroy badly infected plants.

Rust
Symptoms: brown concentric rings appear on pelargonium leaf undersides.
Treatment: remove and burn badly infected leaves; spray or dust with fungicide; improve ventilation; do not take cuttings from infected plants.

Sooty mould
Symptoms: unsightly black mould on honeydew deposited by various insects, blocking leaf pores and exposure to sunlight.
Treatment: spray against pests producing honeydew; wipe off mould with a damp cloth, then rinse off with clean water.

Virus
Symptoms: many, including stunted or distorted growth; pale yellow spots, streaks or patches on leaves; white-streaked flowers.
Treatment: there is no cure, so discard and destroy infected plants as soon as diagnosed; eradicate sap-sucking pests that spread virus.

Top Patio Plants

Enhance your patio all year round with attractive flowering and foliage plants that thrive in its warmth and shelter.

Some garden centres have sections devoted to patio plants – a relatively new marketing term – but any attractive, compact, undemanding plant is fine. Try to include evergreens and colourful foliage plants as well as seasonal flowering plants in your display for year-round interest. Many foliage house plants, herbs, flowering house plants and conservatory plants will also thrive on a sunny patio.

Busy Lizzie (*Impatiens* hybrids)
Size: 15-45 x 15-45cm (6-18 x 6-18in)
Feature: spurred white, pink, orange, red or purple, single or double flowers in summer; plain or variegated leaves; branching, shrubby growth
Position: sun or light shade
Basic care: feed and water freely in spring and summer; prune to keep compact; bring indoors or discard before the first frost
Watchpoints: slugs and greenfly can be problems; overwatering causes rotting

Fuchsia (*Fuchsia* varieties and hybrids)
Size: 15-90 x 15-90cm (6-36 x 6-36in)
Feature: bell-shaped, pendent, white, pink lilac, red or bi-coloured, single or double flowers in summer; plain or variegated, deciduous leaves; shrubby growth; can be trained as standards; weeping forms ideal for hanging baskets
Position: sun or light shade
Basic care: feed and water freely in spring and summer; water sparingly in winter; protect tender forms from frost; prune lightly in spring
Watchpoints: over- or under-watering, greenfly and whitefly can be problems; golden-leaved varieties can scorch in full sun

Patio rose (*Rosa* hybrids)
Size: 30-45 x 30-45cm (12-18 x 12-18in)
Feature: single or double, sometimes fragrant flowers in pink, red, orange, yellow or white, in summer; shrubby growth
Position: sun
Basic care: feed and water freely in spring and summer; water sparingly in autumn and winter; deadhead regularly; cut back by half and mulch in early spring
Watchpoints: greenfly, mildew and blackspot can be problems

Box (*Buxus sempervirens* varieties)
Size: 15-120 x 10-90cm (6-48 x 4-36in)
Feature: small, glossy, evergreen, plain or variegated, pointed, oval or rounded leaves; shrubby growth; can be clipped into topiary forms
Position: sun or light shade
Basic care: feed and water freely in spring and summer; water sparingly in autumn and winter; clip in early, mid and late summer
Watchpoints: box suckers can attack young leaves, causing distorted, cabbage-like growth; cut out plain-leaved shoots on variegated forms as soon as seen

Camellia (*Camellia* species and varieties)
Size: 90-180 x 60-120cm (3-6 x 2-4ft)
Feature: shiny evergreen leaves; single or double, white, pink or red, rose-like flowers from autumn to spring, according to type; shrubby growth
Position: sun or light shade
Basic care: feed and water freely in spring and summer; water sparingly in autumn and winter; mulch in spring; deadhead; prune lightly after flowering, if necessary to control growth
Watchpoints: provide lime-free, ericaceous potting compost; water daily in hot weather

Hosta (*Hosta* species and varieties)
Size: 5-90 x 5-90cm (2-36 x 2-36in)
Feature: rosettes of narrow, oval or heart-shaped, plain or variegated, deciduous leaves, some with deeply set veins and midribs; spikes of white or mauve, lily-like flowers in summer; clump-forming
Position: sun or light shade
Basic care: feed and water generously in spring and summer; water sparingly in autumn and winter; cut back stems after flowering; mulch in spring
Watchpoints: slugs and snails can be a problem

Agapanthus (*Agapanthus* 'Headbourne hybrids')
Size: 60-75 x 38-45cm (24-30 x 15-18in)
Feature: round heads of trumpet-shaped blue flowers in summer and autumn followed by attractive seed heads; strap-shaped, deciduous leaves; clump-forming
Position: sun
Basic care: feed and water generously in spring and summer, water sparingly in autumn and winter; cut back stems after flowering; protect with a thick mulch from frost
Watchpoints: free-draining soil essential; once planted, resents root disturbance

Ivy (*Hedera* species and varieties)
Size: 15-180 x 15-180cm (6-72 x 6-72in)
Feature: evergreen, oval or lobed, glossy, plain or variegated leaves; self-clinging, climbing or trailing growth; mature growth is woody and branching, and carries clusters of green flowers followed by clusters of black berries
Position: sun or light or deep shade
Basic care: provide support initially, eventually self clinging; feed and water freely in spring and summer; water sparingly in autumn and winter; prune in spring or late summer
Watchpoints: scale insects and leaf spot can be problems

SPRING BULBS

*Make the most of the intense colour, heady fragrance and
seasonal beauty of spring-flowering bulbs by displaying them on the patio
or in other spots where they can be readily enjoyed.*

Hardy spring bulbs such as tulips, daffodils and hyacinths are a delight when in bloom. Displayed massed in containers on the patio or other spot close to the house, they can be enjoyed from inside the house as well as from the garden.

Bulbs are cheapest if you buy them dormant in autumn. Garden and DIY centres and larger high street stores stock popular types, often with special discounts for bulk buys and mixed varieties. Specialist nurseries offer a wider selection through bulb catalogues. Costliest but instantly effective are ready planted bulbs in bud or flower; available in spring,

the bulbs can be repotted into different containers.

Plant dormant bulbs in a well crocked, frostproof flowerpot or other container filled with nutrient rich, loam-based potting compost, in early or mid-autumn. As a general guide, cover the bulbs with twice their own height of compost; for the most effective display, plant them close together but not touching. Place them in a sheltered, sunny spot outdoors. Keep them barely moist and protect from severe frost by lagging the containers or by bringing them into a cold but frost-free sunny spot. Once active growth commences, water and feed regularly.

This tiered late-spring medley features toning terracotta and earthenware pots, each planted with a single variety of tulip, hyacinth or narcissi, with pansies, hostas and dwarf conifer and sunflowers for contrast.

COLOUR SCHEMES

Planting a container with a single variety is always elegant, especially if you over-plant – plant the bulbs closer together than normally recommended. The result is a dense mass of colour, even seen from some distance away. Consider extending the scheme to include nearby window boxes or even open ground – a border edging a patio, for example. If you want a multi-coloured effect, combine several containers, each planted with a different coloured variety.

Choose the containers with attention to colour and form – simple, stable shapes always look good, in natural materials rather than plastic. The containers can add a strong element of colour to the scheme or be neutral, allowing the flowers to steal the show. Like the flowers within each container, tightly massing the containers – at ground level, on a bench, table or tiered display stand – is much more effective than loosely dotting them about.

◀ *Mixed planting in one container, such as heathers, pansies, hyacinths and polyanthus, or narcissi, violets and hyacinths, can be charming but place this sort of arrangement where they can be seen up close, such as on a low wall.*

▲ *This impressive trio of spring flowers includes massed white hyacinths, mauve pansies and bright blue grape hyacinths. The bulb bowls add a designer touch.*

◀ *Restrained use of flower colour and attractive terracotta and stoneware containers make a bold statement. If you use bulb bowls without drainage holes, water with extreme care: overwatering can be fatal.*

POTS ON THE PATIO

Bring your garden a little closer to home with plant-filled patio pots and create a colourful, leafy setting for eating out, entertaining or just soaking up the sun.

Patio plants – compact, easy to grow and colourful – are the latest fashion in gardening, with whole sections of garden centres devoted to their display and sales. Though it is only natural to think first about the choice of plants for your patio, the choice of the pots that contain them is equally important.

You may want an understated effect, with traditional plain terracotta pots, or decide on more ornate stylish pots that are decorative in their own right. Some pots feature bas relief, while others are glazed, with or without hand-painted motifs, or highly coloured. If you choose white pots, bear in mind that they may stand out too obviously against the patio background and are quick to show dirt.

Consider also the style of your patio – modern, traditional or Mediterranean, for example – when choosing pots, but try to suit the pots to the plants they are to contain as well. Clematis, for instance, need deep pots to keep the roots cool, while alpines and succulents require wide, shallow ones. Trailing plants such as ivy and lobelia can totally conceal their containers, while upright plants such as hostas and New Zealand flax fully reveal theirs.

Siting pots is important, especially where space is limited. Instead of a fence or balustrade, use a row of substantial pots with tall-growing plants, such as sweet peas, or dwarf box or conifers to edge the patio. You could mark the entrance to the patio from the garden or house with a pair of pots, or use the warmth and shelter of a corner spot to create a feature of several pots.

An old wooden beer-barrel half, with its metal hoops and silvery weather-worn tones, complements the grey brick patio and adds a timeless traditional touch. The barrel is raised on bricks to ensure good drainage, with the bonus of bringing the pansies slightly closer to eye level.

CHOOSING POTS

Garden centres carry a wide range of pots. You can go for a mix and match effect, but keeping to a theme – all terracotta pots, for example, or identical glazed Oriental pots in several sizes – creates a more unified look. You can display pots or decorative outer containers sold for indoor use on the patio, but they may be vulnerable to accidental knocks and weather, especially frost.

Not all garden pots are frost-proof, so check before buying if you intend to leave them out all year round.

Plastic pots are cheap and handy, but for the choice position of a patio, glazed or unglazed terracotta, stone or reproduction stone and wood containers look better and, being heavy, are more stable.

If you already have pots in the garden, patio pots can help to continue the theme.

Try to have at least one large pot. It's easier to look after plants in large pots than small ones, which dry out more quickly and expose the roots to overheating and frost. Large pots also provide a focal point for a cluster of small pots and the opportunity to combine shrubs, climbers and flowers for a genuine container garden.

◀ *Large well proportioned pots – especially if handmade – add to a patio's charm, whether empty or plant filled. This old pitted Ali-baba style pot, with its chips and cracks, marks the transition between patio paving and border.*

◣ *A simple, oval-shaped terracotta pot contains an equally unfussy spring display of tulips. Once the flowers finish, the tulip bulbs can be dried and stored, and the pot filled with summer annuals.*

◀ *Though no longer cheap, an old chimney pot makes a lovely patio planter. Fill it with a drainage layer of gravel or crocks and potting compost, then plant it up. Alternatively, slip a suitably sized ready-planted flower pot into the top. This chimney pot features tobacco plants, marigolds and grey-leaved Helichrysum petiolare.*

▼ *A large shallow pot is ideal for a scaled-down patio herb garden within easy reach of the kitchen. Here golden, lemon-scented and variegated thymes form a geometric pattern around a micro-standard topiary box tree.*

ADDING STYLE

Positioning a collection of pots in a corner is a good way to add interest to a patio. Choose pots in different sizes or materials and plant them up with a selection of plants that show each other off to advantage. To achieve a lush, well established look, plant ground-level patio pots with tall plants such as bamboos, climbers or small standard trees, or display the pots at different heights. A table – old-fashioned sewing-machine tables are ideal – can elevate moderately sized plant-filled pots closer to eye level. The space underneath then provides dappled shade for pots of ferns and ivies.

You can buy antique or reproduction Victorian tiered plant stands, flat-backed or corner-shaped, or simply raise a wooden plank on bricks or concrete blocks – with ivies trailing over the ends, the supports are soon hidden. Wall-hung half pots are always good for high-level interest. You can even buy specially designed pots to clip on to downpipes.

▶ *Enhance wide steps leading to a patio with a single or double row of plant-filled pots. Where patio walls start, end or form corners are similarly first-class locations for one or more pots.*

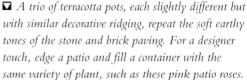

▼ *A trio of terracotta pots, each slightly different but with similar decorative ridging, repeat the soft earthy tones of the stone and brick paving. For a designer touch, edge a patio and fill a container with the same variety of plant, such as these pink patio roses.*

▲ *Shallow, terracotta half-pots – known as alpine pans – and sink gardens filled with rockery plants are ideal on a sunny patio. The gravel adds textural interest and improves drainage. This collection features sempervivums – slow-growing, rosette-forming, hardy succulents.*

Why not plant a medley of vegetables in one container? Pick crops that benefit from the same care regime. Here, a tub is filled with cabbage, celery and melon.

CROP POTS

Even with very little space, you can enjoy the beauty as well as the fresh taste of vegetables and soft fruits by growing specially bred, compact and colourful patio crops in a range of containers.

One of summer's delights is being able to eat your own home-grown vegetables and soft fruits, but few gardens are large enough to incorporate a traditional vegetable plot. Luckily, plant breeders have produced compact, resilient, heavy-cropping varieties, ideal for growing in containers. Often marked as 'patio varieties', they can be grown from seed or bought as young plants from garden centres.

Most are tender, so don't buy young plants until well into spring or put them out until all danger of frost is past, ideally hardening them off first by placing them out on warm days and bringing them in at night. Choose a sunny, sheltered spot on a patio, in a window box, or on a windowsill in a sunny porch or cool room.

You can use growing bags, but terracotta or plastic pots or wooden tubs, 20cm (8in) or more across, are more decorative. Place a layer of drainage material in the base. Loam-based potting composts are ideal as they dry out slowly and help balance heavy crops.

Follow the instructions on the seed packet or care label. As a general guide, keep the potting compost moist, and feed regularly with dilute liquid all-purpose fertilizer or one formulated for leafy crops such as lettuce, or for fruit crops such as tomatoes, peppers and aubergines. Check regularly for any signs of pests or disease and treat as necessary. Some plants may need the growing tips pinched out to encourage the crop, while tall-growing varieties may need support.

▲ *Runner beans planted in a copper pot are a delightful addition to a patio, roof garden or even a balcony. Keep runner beans well watered and fed, and pick the pods as they ripen for a long season of flowers and fruit.*

◀ *Create a temporary summer screen with a row of cordon tomatoes, perfect for edging a patio. Choose an outdoor variety, provide canes and tie in as necessary. Tomatoes crop best if started in a fertilizer rich in nitrogen, then switched to a potash-rich one once the fruits start to develop.*

▲ *Traditionally grown in the ground, grapes can be grown in pots, but need careful watering and feeding. Make sure you pick an outdoor variety for the patio.*

CROPS FOR CONTAINERS

Some plants are more suited to container growing than others. Below are some reliable favourites:

Aubergine	Lettuce
Courgette	Pea
Cucumber	Strawberry
Dwarf bean	Sweet pepper
French bean	Tomato

◀ *Some like it hot and, if you do, these highly decorative chilli peppers are perfect for Chinese, Mexican, Thai or Indian recipes. Dry or pickle those you don't use fresh.*

▶ *The strawberries in this pot give a pretty ruff around a clump of upright lilies. In the spring the strawberry flowers ensure floral interest before the lilies start to bloom.*

Fruit Trees in Containers

Grow compact fruit trees in containers and you can treat yourself to crisp, juicy fruit, picked still warm from the sun – while at the same time enhancing your patio or garden.

Fruit trees in containers are a traditional element of ornamental garden design going back to classical Roman times, as the spring blossom that precedes their summer and autumn fruit ensures an eye-catching display for months on end.

There is a huge variety of fruit trees that lend themselves to containerized growing. Check with your nursery to make sure you choose ones on very dwarfing rootstocks – bush trees on short trunks, branchless columnar trees which fruit on spurs growing directly from the main trunk, old-fashioned fans and family trees with branches of different varieties grafted on to one trunk to ensure pollination and provide a choice of flavours are all good candidates.

Sizes vary, but count on 1.5 x 1m (5 x 3ft) for hardy fruit, half that for citrus trees. Bear in mind that you can hard prune the trees to keep them within bounds, while container growing tends to have a dwarfing effect anyway. Larger garden centres carry the most popular varieties; specialist nurseries sell a wider range, including unusual and old-fashioned varieties – many have a mail order service.

Grow the the fruit trees in well crocked terracotta pots or wooden tubs for stability and appearance. These should be at least 30cm (12in) in diameter, ideally more. Fill the container with a nutrient-rich, loam-based potting compost, then plant the tree and stake it. Keep the tree well watered in spring, summer and early autumn and barely damp in winter. Feed it with dilute liquid fertilizer when the fruits are swelling. Maintenance prune in winter, removing dead, diseased and crossing branches.

Branchless columnar apple trees are ideal for growing in a pot on the patio, as they require a minimum of space and cast very little shade.

TROUBLE-SHOOTING GUIDE

A little know-how before you buy and care once planted will help ensure healthy plants.

❖ Unless a variety is self-fertile – all figs, Morello cherry or Victoria plum, for example – you need a nearby second variety that flowers at the same time for cross pollination to occur.

❖ Always ask for suitable pollinators before buying: the supplier will advise, or information is on the label. Peaches need hand pollinating.

❖ Lag containers with sacking or polythene to protect roots if prolonged frost threatens, or move the trees to a cool frost-free spot indoors.

❖ Varieties vary in their specific pruning needs according to whether they fruit on new or old wood. Ask before buying.

❖ Net the trees, if necessary, to protect buds and fruit from birds, and watch for pests and diseases and treat as soon as seen.

▶ *Fig trees, with their sculptural growth habit and large handsome leaves, are as valuable ornamentally as they are for their fruit. Figs crop best if their roots are restricted; in cool temperate climates, small immature fruits must overwinter on the tree to mature during their second summer.*

◣ *Glossy leaves, scented flowers and showy fruits make the lemon a year-round feature. Eighteenth century orangeries, the forerunners of modern greenhouses, were developed to overwinter containerized citrus trees. Unless your garden is mild and sheltered, overwinter lemon trees in a cool, frost-free spot.*

▲ *Peaches, like nectarines and apricots, need hot summers and autumns to fruit well. All benefit from the heat and shelter of a sunny patio, and can be overwintered in a cool greenhouse.*

◣ *Apple trees, like most containerized fruit, benefit from repotting in fresh compost every two years in early winter. You can prune the tips of leading shoots in summer to keep plants tidy.*

HERBS FOR THE PATIO

Attractive, aromatic and easy-to-grow, herbs in containers are perfect for the patio. Just a step or two away from the kitchen, their delicious, fresh flavours are instantly ready for use.

Pots of herbs make a charming and rewarding addition to a patio, providing subtle colouring and fragrance, as well as handy fresh flavourings for your cooking. The flowers of sweet scented rosemary, sage and thyme attract bees and butterflies to the patio but ward off unwanted insects such as flies.

Choose herbs that you like the look and taste of, checking first that their requirements for light are compatible with the conditions on your patio. Most herbs prefer a sunny position. In the absence of a patio, a light, sunny windowsill is an ideal location for growing fresh herbs.

The containers – pots, tubs, troughs or window boxes – are very much part of the picture. Unless you already have attractive containers, buy small terracotta pots to hold single plants or larger pots or tubs for miniature herb gardens. Set large containers in position before planting up, because they will be too heavy to move afterwards. Look out for unusual containers, like an old ceramic sink, a chimney pot or metal tubs.

Since many herbs have unspectacular flowers, they look good in colourful frost-proof glazed pots. Take delicate herbs indoors in autumn to protect them from early frosts.

Pots are as much a part of a patio display as the herbs they contain. Here terracotta pots, subtly coloured in harmonious rich blue, green and pink tones, make up for the relative lack of flowers on the plants.

PLANTING HERBS IN POTS

In spring or early summer, garden centres carry fresh stocks of young potted herb plants at reasonable prices. Buy a good selection. For contrast, include variegated or coloured-leaf forms, such as golden marjoram or purple basil.

To plant up a new herb, clean the chosen pot thoroughly, and place a layer of coarse gravel in the bottom. Add medium-rich, loam-based potting compost to within 2.5cm (1in) of the top and firm it down. Before re-potting the plant, soak it in water, then gently tease the roots free at the base and round the sides. Stand the plant upright in the new pot and fill in round the sides with potting compost to just below the rim. For a mixed planting, position the central plant first, surrounding it with a little compost to support it while you plant up the other herbs round it. Then fill in with compost as before.

Arrange the herbs carefully, whether they are in individual pots or planted together. Build up a landscape in miniature, perhaps with a shrubby herb such as bay, rosemary or lavender in the centre with smaller types like marjoram, sage, thyme or chives ranged about it and a creeping thyme round the edge. (Spreading varieties like mint are best confined to a pot of their own.) Alternatively, put the larger herbs against a wall to fill a corner.

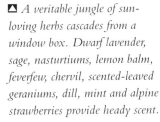

A veritable jungle of sun-loving herbs cascades from a window box. Dwarf lavender, sage, nasturtiums, lemon balm, feverfew, chervil, scented-leaved geraniums, dill, mint and alpine strawberries provide heady scent.

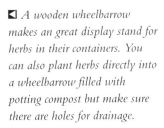

A wooden wheelbarrow makes an great display stand for herbs in their containers. You can also plant herbs directly into a wheelbarrow filled with potting compost but make sure there are holes for drainage.

Mixed culinary and ornamental herbs including golden feverfew, golden thyme, chives, parsley, rue and lady's mantle fill green-glazed cachepots on a tiled patio table creating an orderly look.

CONTAINER CARE

Water the plants regularly, without letting the compost become waterlogged, and feed them with liquid fertilizer every fortnight.

❖

Turn the pots once a week, so that all the plants get their fair share of sun.

❖

Plucking leaves often encourages new growth but remember, overenthusiastic cropping may kill off plants.

❖

Gravel or pebbles covering the surface of the potting compost make an attractive and water-retaining finish.

TERRACOTTA HERB POT

Traditionally used to grow strawberries, a tall terracotta pot with pockets in the side is an ideal and highly decorative container for growing an assortment of fresh herbs on a patio.

A collection of your favourite herbs, each one growing happily out of a separate pocket of an old-fashioned strawberry pot, makes an attractive addition to your patio. Certain small herbs are well suited to this kind of planting, particularly the many varieties of thyme. When planting different herbs together in one pot, you should choose types that have similar requirements for light and water. Basil, sweet marjoram and summer savory are a good combination, as they all need to be brought indoors in the colder months and then moved out on to the patio in the summer.

A strawberry pot filled with herbs always looks impressive, with the colours of the plants showing up well against the red-brown of the terracotta. For a more Mediterranean look, you can whitewash the pot before planting the herbs.

A deep pot like this is large enough to provide the herbs with a healthy growing environment – even deeper rooting herbs like coriander flourish. Remember, the greater the space a herb has for roots the more it will grow, which is important if you are planning to harvest the leaves for cooking.

Perennial herbs like rosemary and sage thrive in pots on a semi-permanent basis; with each year's new growth, they tumble more and more appealingly out of the pockets and down the sides of the pot. If you trim and thin them out annually, they can last several years. Alternatively, you can plant the pot with annual herbs each spring, choosing a different selection every year.

For an attractive symmetry on the patio, you can plant two pots and stand one on either side of the door leading into the house. If you vary the types of herbs you grow in each, you give yourself a greater choice to use in your cooking.

This attractive terracotta strawberry pot is put to good use growing a range of culinary herbs. Parsley fills the top of the pot, with rosemary, thyme and chives in the side pockets.

PLANTING UP A TERRACOTTA HERB POT

Many herbs come from hot, dry climates, so good drainage is essential to keep the compost aerated and unwaterlogged and prevent roots rotting in constantly wet soil. The depth of the strawberry pot allows excess water to drain away well, as long as you put a layer of terracotta crocks or gravel at the bottom of the pot, below the compost, and stand a wire netting tube filled with drainage material down the centre of the pot.

1 Lining the base Place a 2.5cm (1in) layer of drainage material such as coarse gravel or crocks of broken terracotta flowerpots in the base of the strawberry pot.

2 Making the drainage column Wearing gardening gloves to protect your hands and using a pair of wire cutters, cut a rectangular piece of chicken wire, 16-25cm (6¼ -10in) wide by the depth of the pot minus 5-7cm (2-2¾in). Roll it into a small wire mesh tube 5-8cm (2-3¼in) in diameter. Place it vertically in the centre of the pot, burying one end in the drainage material and adjusting the top, if necessary, to come 5-7cm (2-2¾in) below the pot rim. Fill the wire netting column with drainage material.

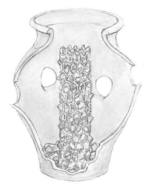

◾ *You don't need to confine your pot to herbs. Here colourful pansies tumble out of the top and sides to give a long-lasting display.*

3 Planting Add potting compost to the pot up to the lowest planting pocket. Working from the outside of the strawberry pot in – or, if the rootball is too big, from the inside out – plant the first herb in the pocket, then water lightly.

4 Filling the pot Continue filling the pot with potting compost, planting and watering until all pockets are full. Add a final layer of potting compost to come 4cm (1½in) below the rim of the pot. Plant one or more herb plants in the top and, if wished, add a gravel mulch for an attractive surface finish. Water well.

HERBS FOR STRAWBERRY POTS

Shrubs and perennials

In the top of the pot:
Bay (*Laurus nobilis*)
Rosemary (*Rosmarinus officinalis*)
Sages (*Salvia officinalis* green species or coloured-leaved varieties 'Purpurascens' and 'Icterina')
Pot marjoram (*Origanum onites*)

In the side pockets:
Chives (*Allium schoenoprasum*)
Common thyme (*Thymus vulgaris*)
Lemon thyme (*Thymus* x *citriodorus*)
Compact marjoram (*Origanum vulgare* 'Compactum')
Creeping savory (*Satureja spicigera*)

Annuals

In the top of the pot:
Sweet basil (*Ocimum basilicum*)
Pot marigold (*Calendula officinalis*)
Chervil (*Anthriscus cerefolium*)
Coriander (*Coriandrum sativum*)
Curled or French parsley (*Petroselinum crispum* varieties)

In the side pockets:
Curled parsley (*Petroselinum crispum*)
French parsley (*Petroselinum crispum* variety)
Bush basil (*Ocimum minimum*)
Summer savory (*Satureja hortensis*)
Nasturtium (*Tropaeolum majus* compact variety)

The Top Ten Herbs for the Patio

For an economical, year-round supply of fresh flavours, try growing these all-time favourites.

Culinary herbs are grown for the flavour or aroma of their leaves – or occasionally of their roots, stems, flowers or seeds. Grown on a patio, their attractive foliage can fill the air with fragrance and, being only a few steps from the house, they are an instantly available ingredient for your cooking and a perfect garnish for a finished dish. The following herbs are easy to please and thrive outdoors in the shelter of a patio.

1 Chives
(*Allium schoenoprasum*)

Uses: salads, soups, sauces, vegetables, fish and poultry
Type: herbaceous perennial, evergreen in mild climates
Size: 15-30cm (6-12in)
Special features: pincushion mauve flowers in summer; giant and garlic flavoured varieties available; grow as a deterrent for aphids, apple scab and mildew
Position: in individual pots or as edging
Basic care: remove faded flowers; lift, divide and replant the clumps every 3-4 years; pick chives for culinary use by snipping leaves at base of plant; remove flowers for better flavour
Special needs: use moisture retentive potting compost

2 Parsley
(*Petroselinum crispum*)

Uses: salads, soups, stews, sauces, stuffings, vegetables, garnishing
Type: biennial or short lived perennial
Size: 20-60 x 15-45cm (8-24 x 6-18in)
Special features: moss-curled varieties have especially attractive foliage
Position: in individual pots or containers; dwarf forms as edging
Basic care: keep well watered in dry weather; pinch out flowerbuds as soon as they appear
Special needs: a rich potting compost and steady supply of water prevent it running to seed prematurely

3 Sage
(*Salvia officinalis*)

Uses: stuffings for poultry, pork and other rich meats
Type: soft-wooded shrub or perennial
Size: up to 60 x 60cm (2 x 2ft), usually smaller
Special features: blue flowers in summer; purple leaved, golden variegated and multi-coloured varieties available
Position: in pots or tubs, singly or in groups
Basic care: prune in spring; water in dry weather; every 3-5 years replace older, leggy plants with young ones
Special needs: free-draining potting compost essential

4 Marjoram
(*Origanum* species)

Uses: meat, poultry, fish, salads, soups, stuffings
Type: herbaceous perennial; grow sweet marjoram as a half-hardy annual
Size: 15-60 x 15-30cm (6-24 x 6-12in)
Special features: tiny pink or white flowers in summer; sweet (knotted) marjoram, pot marjoram, golden variegated and golden leaved marjoram available
Position: in individual pots; compact forms as edging in sink gardens or in cracks between paving slabs
Basic care: pinch out tips to encourage branching; cut back above ground growth in autumn and protect roots against prolonged frost. Sow in spring and divide in spring or autumn
Special needs: Use well drained, nutrient rich potting compost; golden leaved forms need light shade

5 Thyme
(*Thymus* species)
Uses: soups, stews, meat, fish and poultry
Type: dwarf, woody, upright or carpet-forming shrublet
Size: up to 30 x 30cm (1 x 1ft) for shrubby types, 2.5 x 30cm (1 x 12in) for creeping varieties
Special features: tiny pink, white or crimson flowers in summer; golden leaved, silver variegated, woolly leaved and lemon scented forms available
Position: in pots or sink gardens; creeping forms in cracks between paving slabs or as edging
Basic care: water in dry weather; prune in spring and after flowering; lift, divide, and replant creeping forms every 3-5 years
Special needs: free-draining potting compost essential

6 Mint
(*Mentha* species)
Uses: sauces, jellies, vegetables, drinks, garnishing
Types: upright or creeping herbaceous perennial **Size:** 2.5-90cm (1-36in), wide spreading
Position: creeping forms in sink gardens, or as edging; stronger growing forms in individual pots or tubs; sun or shade equally suitable
Basic care: water generously in dry weather; cut back above ground in autumn; lift, divide and replant every 3-4 years
Special needs: use rich, moisture retentive potting compost

7 Bay
(*Laurus nobilis*)
Uses: stews, soups, casseroles, sauces and milk puddings
Type: slow-growing evergreen shrub
Size: up to 120 x 90cm (4 x 3ft) in containers
Special features: standard 'lollipop', flame-shaped topiary and golden leaved forms available
Position: as topiary specimen in container or in mixed herb tub
Basic care: water regularly in spring and summer
Special needs: lag container to protect from prolonged frost or move indoors to a cold, light spot; protect from wind, which can turn leaves brown

8 Sweet basil
(*Ocimum basilicum*)
Uses: tomatoes, salads, sauces, herb vinegars, pasta dishes
Type: half-hardy annual
Size: 20-60cm (8-24in)
Special features: purple leaved, bush and lemon scented forms available
Basic care: keep well watered; remove any flowerbuds and pinch out growing tips frequently to encourage bushy growth
Special needs: protect from wind; mist-spray leaves in hot weather; take in before first frost and grow on a cool, sunny windowsill indoors

9 Rosemary
(*Rosmarinus officinalis*)
Uses: stuffings, roasts, stews, marinades, herb vinegars
Type: slow-growing evergreen shrub
Size: up to 1 x 1m (3 x 3ft) in containers
Special features: blue, white or pink flowers in early summer; a low-growing, prostrate variety available
Position: in a mixed herb tub or trailing over a wall
Basic care: water regularly in spring and summer
Special needs: lag container to protect from prolonged frost or move indoors to a cold, light spot; free-draining potting compost essential

10 French tarragon
(*Artemisia dracunculus*)
Uses: chicken, fish, seafood, sauces, herb vinegar
Type: herbaceous perennial
Size: 60 x 45cm (24 x 18in)
Special features: tiny flowers in hot summers
Position: at the back of a group of containers or against a wall
Basic care: water only in dry weather; pinch out growing tips frequently to promote bushy growth; cut back above ground growth in autumn; lift and divide every 3-4 years
Special needs: use well drained, potting compost, low in nutrients; lag container to protect from prolonged frost or move indoors to a cool, light spot

10

PICKING HERBS

Leaves are most intensely flavoured just before flowering. To ensure an ongoing supply of young leaves, pick sparingly, choosing one or two sprigs from each plant; never strip a plant bare. With rosette-forming plants such as parsley, pick older, outer sprigs, leaving the young central shoots to develop.

5

6

7

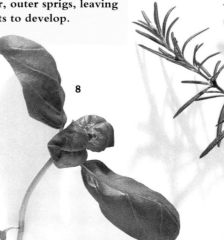

8

9

Seasonal Hanging Baskets

With flower-filled hanging baskets, you can easily add bright splashes of seasonal colour to your patio or garden in spring, autumn and winter as well as summer.

H anging baskets are an easy option for quick colour, especially where garden space is limited. Even without a garden you can enhance a porch, front door or window with a dense, dazzling display of flowers and foliage. Though hanging baskets are traditionally filled with summer annuals and bedding plants, a little planning lets you make them cheerful garden features all year round. If you like, you can plant up two or three baskets designed to flower in sequence. If you do this it helps to have somewhere in the garden to keep long-term plants when they are out of season.

For a colourful display until autumn, plant hanging baskets with summer flowers such as fuchsias, lobelias, begonias, geraniums and petunias after the last spring frost. You can over-winter these plants in a cool but frost-free spot such as a greenhouse, unheated spare room or shed, until next spring.

For late autumn, winter and early spring colour, use dwarf evergreen shrubs such as skimmia, box, conifer or ivy, and winter-flowering plants like pansies, polyanthus and cyclamen.

Plan ahead for spring colour by planting biennials, such as wallflowers and forget-me-nots, and dormant bulbs, such as daffodils or tulips, in early autumn. Keep the basket in a sheltered, sunny, out-of-the-way spot while your winter basket is on show. Or, buy bulbs and biennials in bud and plant the basket in spring. Plants in bud cost more and require careful handling, but the results can be just as attractive.

A host of golden daffodils fills a moss-lined hanging basket for an enchanting spring display. To achieve the spherical, tiered floral effect plant the bulbs in layers, placing lower bulbs angled outwards round the basket's edge. Finish with a closely-packed, all-over top layer of bulbs.

◀ *For a winter focal point as colourful as any summer display, combine pink-budded, evergreen skimmia, variegated ivy, winter-flowering pansies, polyanthus and heathers. Fresh conifer clippings – an unusual alternative to sphagnum moss – line the basket, concealing the polythene inner lining and providing an interesting and inexpensive designer touch.*

T I P

LOOKING AFTER YOUR BASKET

Hanging baskets are densely planted for maximum effect, so they have relatively little root space. To ensure that the plants thrive, feed and water them regularly during the growing season. Use a potash-rich fertilizer such as tomato fertilizer for a hanging basket in full flower and be prepared to give a summer hanging basket in full sun a daily and sometimes even a twice-daily watering.

▲ *For an eye-catching summer hanging basket with edible as well as ornamental value, combine compact herbs and colourful, quick-growing vegetables such as parsley and dwarf tomatoes. Plant in late spring, after the last frost, and harvest regularly but sparingly to maintain the display, while enjoying the fruits of your labour at the same time.*

◀ *You can bring even the dreariest pebble-dashed wall to life with a blaze of summer colour. This half-basket contains fuchsias, petunias, geraniums, tuberous-rooted begonias, ivies, creeping Jenny, busy Lizzies and marigolds. Plants in half-baskets benefit from the shelter and latent heat of a wall, giving more lavish displays here than elsewhere.*

Preparing a Hanging Basket

Careful preparation and planting is the key to a long-lasting and attractive display of plants in a hanging basket.

A hanging basket, filled with a mass of flowers, is the perfect way to soften the severe lines of an outside wall or to add a decorative touch to a porchway. In order to achieve an effective display, it is important to prepare the container properly and to think carefully about where to position it.

Types of basket

When choosing a basket for hanging, bear in mind that it needs to be fairly lightweight. Once you have added the soil and plants, you don't want it to be too heavy to pick up.

Round hanging baskets For traditional round shapes, the commercial wire holders, coated in green, white or black plastic, are ideal. As well as being lightweight, they are also inexpensive and easy to plant. Solid plastic containers are another low-cost option, but the plastic sides are difficult to conceal as the plants cannot grow through the base. Wicker baskets and wooden buckets look pretty, but may not last longer than one season. You can always improvise with a wire salad basket or an old colander.

Wall baskets, which have either flat backs so that you can attach them to a vertical surface easily or pointed backs designed to fit into a corner, are also good for displaying hanging plants. Terracotta, ceramic and wrought-iron designs are practical and attractive. For planting on a larger scale, an iron hay-feeding basket looks very effective fixed on to a brick wall.

Position

Always consider the viewing height for the hanging basket before you hang it up. A moss-lined basket with a good display of flowers on top and a few plants trailing down the sides looks best at eye level, whereas a ball of flowers can hang quite high up as the base is covered in plants.

Make sure that you site the basket where you can water it easily – for a high-level basket, a self-locking pulley for raising and lowering it is a good idea. Remember, too, not to position the basket where dripping might cause a problem, or where the growing plants obstruct an entrance. Choose a sheltered, sunny or semi-shaded spot for best results and try to keep the basket well away from passing traffic.

Attachments

For hanging round baskets, buy strong metal wall brackets with the bracket arm longer than the basket radius, so that it hangs freely. Secure the bracket firmly to a wall with screws and wallplugs or to a sturdy beam on a pergola or porch. Use the chains provided to suspend the basket, or buy wire or nylon instead.

Planting a hanging basket

Summer is the most popular season for hanging baskets, largely because there is a good range of suitable annuals that keep on flowering profusely all season long. Finding plants that maintain the same vigorous growth during the winter is more difficult. Ivy is a reliable partner for winter-flowering pansies or early primroses or daffodils in the spring, for example, while fuchsias prolong the flowering into the autumn.

For a summer-long display, plant up the hanging basket in mid to late spring with a selection of plants, keeping a balance of colourful flowers and foliage. Remember to allow space for growth – the plants grow remarkably quickly and soon fill out the basket with a profusion of colour. It's a good idea to include a few bushy, flowery types – like zoned pelargoniums, busy Lizzies, begonias and pansies – in the centre to create a rounded top to the display. Trailing plants – such as lobelia, nasturtiums, verbena and weeping fuchsia – tumble down the sides creating an overflowing-basket effect.

Lining the basket

All baskets have to be lined before planting. One of the easiest ways to line a wire basket is to use a pre-formed liner which is made from compressed peat, textile fibre and wood pulp. A lining of moss is the most attractive option, but you have to add a layer of plastic sheeting or coarse sacking between the moss and soil in order to retain moisture. Sphagnum or carpet moss is the best type to use and is readily available from garden centres.

1 Preparing the moss lining Place the basket on a bucket, then line it with a 15mm (⅝in) thick layer of moss, so it totally covers the inside of the basket.

2 Lining with plastic Cut a piece of plastic sheeting to fit and place it over the moss. Press into place and trim to neaten. If you are not growing plants through the base, cut five drainage holes in the plastic around the basket.

TIP

PINNED DOWN

To encourage stems to grow down over the edge of the basket, you can fix them in place round the sides with fine hairpins stuck into the compost.

3 Adding trailing plants Cover the base of the basket with potting compost. Just above the compost, make a ring of holes in the lining, then poke the plant roots through the holes from the outside. Cover with a layer of compost. Thread through more trailing plants until you are about 10cm (4in) from the top.

4 Planting the middle top Cover the last layer of trailing plants with potting compost to within 2.5cm (1in) of the rim. Plant the tallest plants in the middle of the top, firming the compost round them to make slight depressions to retain moisture after watering.

CARE OF PLANTS

When planting a hanging basket, you use a lightweight potting mixture which drains and dries out quickly, so you need to water regularly – once or even twice a day in hot weather. Mist plants in the evening in prolonged heat waves. Feed with diluted liquid fertilizer every two weeks in spring and summer, and remove faded blooms to extend the flowering period. If the soil becomes too dry, you may find that watering is not effective, because the water is not absorbed into the soil. In which case, take down the basket and lower it into a tub of water. Leave until the soil is well soaked, then lift out and allow the excess water to drain away before rehanging.

5 Completing the basket Plant trailers around the rim of the basket, making sure that the stems hang well over the edge to encourage them to grow downwards. With the basket still in place over the bucket, water thoroughly with a fine spray. Allow excess water to drain away before hanging it up.

Preparing a Window Box

Whether you live in the country or in town, a window box will enhance your home from both inside and out.

A window box is one of the easiest ways to give a lift to the outside of a house. If you live in a house with a garden, you can enliven the frontage with a cheerful mix of flowering and foliage plants. For many city dwellers, a window box is probably the nearest they get to having their own garden, and a careful choice of planting can go a long way to brightening up the urban scene.

Whether you decide to replant as the seasons come and go, opt for long-term interest or combine seasonal and more permanent planting, it's essential to choose the right sort of window box and prepare it carefully. Plants in the confined space of a window box need extra care if they are to thrive – nothing looks more forlorn than straggly plants in poorly drained, unsuitable containers.

With a little extra effort over preparation, your plants will get off to a good start and continue to flourish and give pleasure for their full lifespan.

Position

Make sure that your window box is accessible; plants in a confined space need frequent watering, so you must be able to water from the garden or open the window and reach outside easily with a watering can or jug.

Have a good sized drip tray so that you do not splash walls, and perhaps windows on lower storeys, when watering. Make sure that surplus water can drain away freely by using special feet – available from garden centres – to raise the container off the drip tray.

A sunny site gives the best results, but don't abandon hope if your window is in a shady spot. Simply choose plants such as box and ivy which are more shade tolerant. The advantage of a shady position is that the window box won't dry out as quickly – always a problem for container plants.

Remember that in a large town or city, the warmth of the buildings raises the outside temperature, so you can grow plants that are relatively tender, such as certain fuchsias.

Materials

Terracotta is the traditional material for containers; providing it is frostproof, it should last for years. It is heavy, so make sure the support is adequate.

Concrete is heavy, but it's long lasting and relatively inexpensive.

Wood gives an attractive natural look, but you need to use a plastic liner, or treat the inside with a horticultural preservative. Protect the exterior with paint or varnish.

Plastic is cheap, lightweight and long lasting. Though it's not as attractive as more traditional materials, you can trail a plant like ivy over the outside, or use a paint effect to soften the finish.

Fibreglass is also fairly inexpensive, as well as being light, strong and durable. Many modern fibreglass window boxes are passable imitations of traditional lead ones.

Lead is expensive and heavy, but very handsome. It's wise to secure a valuable container against theft – large garden centres sell chains that can be inserted through the drainage hole and secured to a wall.

Thorough preparation is the key to success for a showy display – keep drainage holes clear with water-retaining clay pebbles, and start plants off with special container compost.

Fixing a window box

Window boxes are extremely heavy once they're filled with drainage material, compost and plants, so make sure your box is well supported and secured.

Don't skimp on the size of your window box – the bigger the box, the more showy the display of planting. Choose a box that is at least 15cm (6in) from front to back and 20cm (8in) deep. This size should hold a fair amount of compost – any smaller will not hold enough moisture or be able to accommodate a reasonable root system.

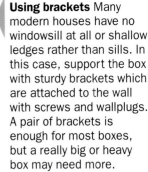

Using brackets Many modern houses have no windowsill at all or shallow ledges rather than sills. In this case, support the box with sturdy brackets which are attached to the wall with screws and wallplugs. A pair of brackets is enough for most boxes, but a really big or heavy box may need more.

Adding style Where the fixings will show, or if you want to make a special feature of them, look for ornamental wrought iron effect brackets which are more attractive than the plain L-shaped versions.

Securing with hooks and eyes A box on a high ledge or windowsill needs to be well secured for safety. An eye-hook screwed into each end of the box, with corresponding long arm hooks (or chains with hooks) screwed into the window frame, gives additional support.

Giving stability If your windowsill slopes, put wedges under the box to keep it level and stop it sliding off.

Preparing for planting

1 Soaking plants While you prepare the window box, stand the plants in their original containers in a bowl of water so that the compost becomes thoroughly wet.

2 Allowing for drainage Most window boxes come complete with drainage holes. If you buy a plastic, fibreglass or wooden version that hasn't already got them, drill or punch holes about 2cm (¾in) in diameter. For a base 1m (3ft) long, two holes are enough.

3 Lining the base Place a few large stones or pebbles in the base and over the drainage holes, then cover these with a layer of water-retaining clay pebbles or coarse gravel. Add two layers of hessian, horticultural fleece or similar material to keep pebbles and compost separate. Finish off with a 5cm (2in) layer of compost.

4 Putting in the plants Tap the plants out of their pots, keeping the rootball intact. Tease out any entwined roots. Position the plants with the base of their stems just below the top of the window box. Firm compost around the plants to about 2.5cm (1in) of the rim. Water thoroughly using a fine spray hose.

CONTAINER COMPOST

Don't economize by using soil from the garden, as it may be too acid or alkaline, and it could harbour pests or diseases. Instead, buy potting compost specially prepared for containers. This usually contains slow-release fertilizer, and is ideal for most window box planting. Certain species, such azaleas and heathers, need special compost.

MAKING A WINDOW BOX

These window boxes will attract as many admiring glances from passers-by as the blooms displayed in them – and you don't need to be a skilled carpenter to make them.

W indow boxes, overflowing with flowers or foliage, can enhance the view from a window and add all-year-round beauty to the outside of your home. You can buy all sorts of plastic and terracotta planters from garden centres, but these handmade wooden versions – with picket fence or log-cabin style trim – are hard to beat, and look good even before spring shoots start to peep above the soil.

Using only a few tools and materials and basic woodworking skills, these window boxes are inexpensive and straightforward to build. The interior framework of the window box is made from exterior grade plywood. This is faced with planed softwood

picket fencing or lengths of rustic pole, and then sealed with a water-tight paint or preservative finish.

When designing your own window box, there are a number of points you need to think about. The box needs to fit comfortably and securely on the window sill and, unless you want to conceal an ugly view, the height of the box and final plant height should not block out all natural light. The style of your home and garden is important too, so the box doesn't look out of place. The box also needs to suit the plants you grow in it; tiny primroses and violets look sweet peeping out of a shallow container but can get lost in a deep box with towering sides.

There's no need to settle for a run-of-the-mill plastic window box when you can make one as charming as this. For a rustic but weatherproof finish, apply two coats of paint in different colours, sand down the top coat to reveal patches of the colour beneath, then seal it with several coats of exterior grade, clear matt varnish.

PICKET FENCE WINDOW BOX

The picket fencing that faces this window box is made from planed softwood, cut into lengths and shaped to a point at one end. The lengths are nailed on to panels of exterior-grade plywood, which are then assembled to make the four sides of the box. The base of the box has drainage holes and is raised slightly on batten supports to prevent the soil inside from becoming waterlogged. If necessary, lift the box off the ground by standing it on a couple of bricks.

To ensure the wood doesn't rot, it's important to seal each piece of timber or plywood with wood primer or horticultural preservative before fixing it to another piece. This means that all the meeting faces are protected from water penetration.

CALCULATING AMOUNTS

Measure the width and depth of the window sill, then decide on the window box size to sit comfortably in this space. You may have to adjust the length (**A**) and width (**B**) slightly to allow for a complete rows of pickets. The window box shown here measures 770 x 240mm (30 x 9½in) and is 250mm (10in) high.
How many pickets? Add together the length of the front, back and sides (2 x **A** + 2 x **B**), then divide by the picket width – 75mm (3¾in).

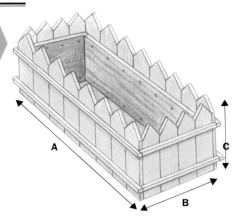

▼ *A picket-fence window box adds country charm to any home. If the window sill is too narrow, support the window box with brackets or stand it on the ground as a free-standing planter, with a couple of bricks underneath to ensure good drainage.*

1 **Cutting the picket pieces** Using a tape measure, try square and panel saw, cut a piece of 19 x 75mm (¾ x 3in) planed timber to the window box height (**C**). Use this as a template for cutting the remaining picket pieces (see *Calculating Amounts*).

2 **Shaping the pickets** Mark a point in the centre of the top end of a picket piece. Then mark a line across the width, 30mm (1¼in) below the end. Join the marks to form a point, then cut off the corners with a panel saw. Use as a template to shape the rest of the pickets. Smooth the cut edges with abrasive paper and seal with a coat of primer or preservative.

3 **Cutting the plywood panels** *For the front and back:* cut two pieces of plywood, each measuring **A** minus 40mm (1½in) x **C** minus 40mm (1½in). *For the sides:* cut two pieces of plywood, each measuring **B** minus 40mm (1½in) x **C** minus 62mm (2⅜in). Seal with primer or preservative.

4 **Attaching the pickets** Using adhesive, stick a row of pickets on to the front and back panels, with the bottom edges flush and with the pickets overlapping beyond the ends of the plywood by 20mm (¾in) at each side. Reinforce each picket with two panel pins hammered through the plywood into the picket. Secure pickets to side panels in the same way, but allow a 12mm (½in) overlap at each end.

5 **Fixing the base supports** Cut two lengths of batten, just shorter than the front panel length. Seal the battens. Drill and countersink 4mm (⁵⁄₃₂in) clearance holes at about 15cm (6in) intervals along the battens. Centre a batten along the inside lower edge of the front and back panels, and transfer the screwhole positions on to the panels with a bradawl. Drill 2mm (³⁄₃₂in) pilot holes at the marks, apply adhesive along the back face of the batten, then secure with 50mm (2in) No 8 countersunk woodscrews.

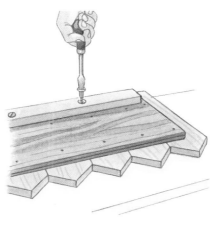

6 **Assembling the box** At both ends of the front and back panels, measure 10mm (⅜in) from the edge and 20mm (¾in) from the top and bottom of the picket and mark these points. Drill and countersink a 4mm (⁵⁄₃₂in) clearance hole at each mark. Hold the meeting edges in position to transfer the drill hole positions on to the edges of the side panels. Drill a 2mm (³⁄₃₂in) pilot hole at each mark. Apply waterproof woodworking adhesive to the meeting edges and screw together using 50mm (2in) No 8 countersunk woodscrews.

7 **Making the base** Cut a plywood rectangle to fit flat inside the box. Drill some evenly spaced, 15-20mm (⅝-¾in) drainage holes in the rectangle. Seal with preservative and fit in place, resting on the supports.

8 **Trimming the box (optional)** Cut and seal two strips of moulding measuring **A** and four strips measuring **B**. Position two strips of moulding at the desired height on the front and each side of the box. Fix in place with waterproof woodworking adhesive and panel pins. Finish with a coat of preservative or two coats of exterior grade paint.

TIP

QUICK CUTTING

If you have a mitre saw or mitre box with a right angle cutting guide that is wide enough to hold 75mm (3in) timber, it's a lot easier and more accurate to use this for cutting the lengths of picket fence.

LOG CABIN WINDOW BOX

The basic plywood framework described on the previous page can be decorated in many different ways. One variation, shown here, is to cover it with lengths of rustic pole. These are available from garden centres, or you could use woody prunings from your own or a neighbour's garden. If you're unable to find enough straight lengths, you could cut shorter pieces and fix them upright around the sides. Other ways to face the box are to use split logs, garden or woven willow fencing and trellis.

YOU WILL NEED

❖ RUSTIC POLES
❖ WBP PLYWOOD, 12mm (½in)
❖ BATTEN, 19 x 25mm (¾ x 1in)
❖ TRY SQUARE
❖ TAPE MEASURE
❖ PANEL SAW
❖ OLD PAINT BRUSH
❖ CLEAR HORTICULTURAL PRESERVATIVE
❖ HAMMER AND GALVANIZED NAILS TO SUIT AVERAGE POLE DIAMETER AND 75mm (3in)

MEASURING UP

To work out the height of the plywood panel for the sides, decide on the approximate height of the window box, then lay rustic poles side by side to achieve this height. Measure the combined widths of the poles and subtract 12mm (½in) to give the panel height (**D**).

The galvanized nails for securing the poles to the plywood panels must be as long as the average pole diameter, plus at least half the thickness of the plywood.

1 Cutting the plywood panels *For the front and back:* measure the diameter of an average sized rustic pole and multiply by two. Subtract this figure from **A** and cut two pieces of plywood to this length by the panel height (**D**). *For the sides:* add together twice the panel thickness plus twice the average pole diameter. Subtract this figure from **B** and cut two plywood panels to this length by **D**. Seal the panels.

☑ *Chestnut poles make an attractive natural facing for this window box that is sure to look good on any window sill. Using unpainted poles also means the box can be filled with every type and colour of flower.*

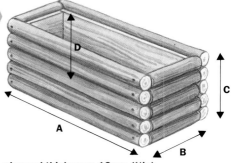

plywood thickness: 12mm (½in)

2 Cutting the rustic poles *For the front and back:* cut a length of rustic pole that measures **A**. Use this as a template for cutting remaining poles to cover the front and back of the box. *For the sides:* cut a length of rustic pole that measures **B** less twice the pole diameter. Use this as a template for cutting remaining poles to cover the sides of the box. Seal with preservative.

3 Attaching the poles Using suitable length galvanized nails, secure the poles to the right plywood panels so the bottom poles are flush with the lower edges; poles overlap by an equal amount at each end and by 12mm (½in) at the top edge.

4 Assembling the box Fix base supports, following step 5, *Picket Fence Window Box*. Hold the front and a side panel together, so front poles overlap the cut edges of the side poles and fix with 75mm (3in) nails. Fix other panels in the same way. Make a plywood base following step 7, *Picket Fence Window Box*. Seal with preservative.

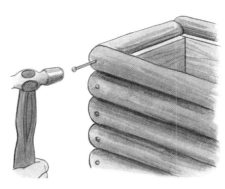

SEASONAL WINDOW BOXES

It's easy to create densely packed, colourful window box displays.
For year round pleasure, each season's planting should follow
smoothly on from the one before.

Colourful window box plants, whether spring bulbs, summer bedding or permanent evergreens such as ivy, can greatly enhance your view of the outside world seen from inside your home, as well as creating a charming welcome when viewed from outside. If you have a garden, window box plants can follow existing schemes or provide a pleasant contrast; if you don't, cheerful window box displays are even more important.

Window boxes are by their nature limited in size, so a relatively small outlay on plants can result in a stunning show. Garden centres offer a wide range of popular compact or dwarf free-flowering plants – many are sold in bud or flower for instant colour. For permanent planting, on their own or as a framework for seasonal plants, choose dwarf forms of evergreen shrubs such as conifers, box, hebe, skimmia, euonymus or ivy.

Most flowering plants bought in bud will put on a decent show in sun or light shade; for deep shade, choose foliage plants such as ferns and ivies. For exposed sites, choose plants with waxy or leathery leaves such as wax begonias, sempervivums or echeverias.

With a permanent planting of dwarf conifers and ivy, this colourful summer scheme makes good use of popular bedding plants such as busy Lizzies (impatiens), trailing lobelia, pelargoniums and fuchsia.

SEASONAL CHOICE

Put the plants in the biggest window box you have room for, and bear in mind that plants in a densely planted window box will need frequent watering and feeding during the growing season.

SPRING

Dormant bulbs and spring biennials such as wallflower can be planted in mid autumn but may look dull over winter, so mix them with winter-flowering plants. Alternatively, pay extra and buy and plant them in flower in spring. After flowering, lift and plant bulbs in the garden or dry off and store for future use.

Spring alternatives

Chionodoxa	Narcissus
Crocus	Pansy
Forget-me-not	Polyanthus
Grape hyacinth	Scilla
Hyacinth	Tulips
Iris reticulata	Wallflower

◢ *Hyacinths and narcissi bring a sweet scented breath of spring to a windowsill. In sheltered situations bulbs will flower earlier than in the open ground.*

SUMMER

Though often on sale earlier, buy summer plants after the last frost. Leave in place until they finish flowering or until the first frost, often mid or late autumn, depending on the weather.

Summer alternatives

African marigold	Marguerites
Ageratum	Nasturtium
Busy Lizzie (*impatiens*)	Miniature rose
Campanula	Pelargonium
Coleus	Petunia
Dahlia	Silver-leaved cineraria
French marigold	Sweet alyssum
Fuchsia	Tobacco plant
Helichrysum petiolare	Tuberous-rooted begonia
Kingfisher daisy	Verbena
Lobelia	Wax begonia

◢ *Busy Lizzies, an azalea and dahlias provide a cheery burst of colour against an evergreen framework on this summer sill. Combining trailing and upright plants in this way makes the most of limited space.*

WINTER

This is the most challenging season but you can still achieve colourful effects with variegated evergreens and hardy flowers such as cyclamen, snowdrops and winter-flowering pansies. In a sheltered spot try cinerarias and azaleas.

Winter alternatives

Azalea	Heather
Chrysanthemum	Pansy
Cineraria	Polyanthus
Crocus	Snowdrop
Cyclamen	Winter aconite

◢ *Combine the mellow colours of winter heathers and ornamental kale with evergreens like skimmia, pieris, ivies and dwarf conifers for a winter-long display.*

Index

ACKNOWLEDGEMENTS

Photographs: 77-8 Robert Harding Syndication/IPC Magazines, 9-10 EM/Simon Page-Ritchie, 11 Ariadne, 12-15 EM/Sue Atkinson, 16 EM/Steve Tanner, 17-18 Period Living and Traditional Homes (Gloria Nicol), 19-26 EM/Sue Atkinson, 27-28 The Garden Picture Library/Lynne Brotchie, 29-30 EM/John Suett, 31 EM/Graham Rae, 32 EM/John Suett, 33 EM/Martin Norris, 34 Insight London, 35, 36(tl) The Garden Picture Library/Linda Burgess, 36(tr) EWA/Spike Powell, (bl) Robert Harding Syndication/IPC Magazines, (br) Insight London, 37-38 Houses and Interiors, 39 Ariadne, 40 Robert Harding Syndication/IPC Magazines, 41, 42(l,tr) The Garden Picture Library/Steven Wooster, 42(br) The Garden Picture Library/Mayer/LeScanff, 43-44 EM/Graham Rae, 45-46 EM/Steve Tanner, 47-50 EM/Sue Atkinson, 51-52 EM/Steve Tanner, 53-56 EM/Sue Atkinson, 57 EM/Simon Page-Ritchie, 58(tl) EM/Adrian Taylor, (r) Robert Harding Syndication/IPC Magazines, (bl) Marie Claire Maison/Dugied/Postic, 59-60 EM/Simon Page-Ritchie, 61-62 Robert Harding Syndication/IPC Magazines, 63(tl) Photos Horticultural, (tr) Jerry Harpur, (c,br) The Garden Picture Library/Lynne Brotchie, (bl) The Garden Picture Library/Vaughan Fleming, 64(tl,br) The Garden Picture Library/Lynne Brotchie, (tr) The Garden Picture Library/Steven Wooster, (c) The Garden Picture Library/Brigitte Thomas, (bl) John Glover, 65-66 EM/Adrian Taylor, 67-68 EM/Sue Atkinson, 69 Worldwide Syndication, 70(bl) EM/Sue Atkinson, (br) The Garden Picture Library/Michèle Lamontagne, 71 EWA/Andreas von Einsiedel, 72 Robert Harding Syndication/IPC Magazines, 73(t) Andrew Lawson, (bl) Clive Nichols, 74(t,bl) Clive Nichols, (br) Photos Horticultural, 75-76 EM/Steve Tanner, 77 John Glover, 78 EM/John Suett, 79(t,b) EM/John Suett, (c) Harry Smith Collection, 80 Harry Smith Collection, 81(t) EM/Graham Rae, (b) EM/John Suett, 82(t) EM/John Suett, (b) EM/Graham Rae, 83 Robert Harding Syndication/IPC Magazines, 84(tl) EWA/Nadia Mackenzie, (bl) EWA, (r) Robert Harding Syndication/IPC Magazines, 85 EWA/Graham Henderson, 86(t,cl,br) Worldwide Syndication, (bl) Robert Harding Syndication/IPC Magazines, 87-94 EM/Steve Tanner, 97(l,c) John Glover, (br) Clive Nichols/Anthony Noel, 98(tl) EWA/Jerry Harpur, (c) Clive Nichols, (b) Andrew Lawson, 99-101 Clive Nichols, 102 Pots and Pithoi, 102-103 Clive Nichols, 104(tr,bl) Clive Nichols, (br) The Garden Picture Library/Jon Bouchier, 105 Harry Smith Collection, 106(tl) Garden and Wildlife Matters, (tr) Andrew Lawson, (c) S&O Mathews, (bl) Sutton Seeds, (br) The Garden Picture Library/Mel Watson, 107 The Garden Picture Library/Stephen Robson, 108(tl) Harry Smith Collection, (tr) EWA/Jay Patrick, (bl) Andrew Lawson, (br) S&O Mathews, 109 The Garden Picture Library/Linda Burgess, 110(t) The Garden Picture Library/Brian Carter, (c) The Garden Picture Library/Lynne Brotchie, (b) The Garden Picture Library/Linda Burgess, 111 EWA/David Lloyd, 112 John Glover, 113 Sue Atkinson, 115 Photos Horticultural, 116(t) The Garden Picture Library/John Glover, (b) Neil Holmes, 117 EM/Steve Tanner, 119 EM/Simon Page-Ritchie, 121 Marie Claire Idées/Broussard/Taralon, 122 Period Living and Traditional Homes, 124 Marie Claire Idées/Broussard/Taralon, 125 The Garden Picture Library/Jon Bouchier, 126(t) EM/John Suett, (c) The Garden Picture Library/Jon Bouchier, (b) John Glover.

Illustrations: Christine Hart-Davies.